MW01067869

DISABILITY, CULTURE, |

Alfredo J. Artiles, ~~Series Editor~~

Affirming Disability

Strengths-Based Portraits
of Culturally Diverse Families

Janet Story Sauer
Zachary Rossetti

Foreword by Maria de Lourdes B. Serpa

TEACHERS COLLEGE PRESS

TEACHERS COLLEGE | COLUMBIA UNIVERSITY
NEW YORK AND LONDON

Published by Teachers College Press, 1234 Amsterdam Avenue, New York, NY 10027

Cover art: "Untitled" by Sachin Arora (see Chapter 5). Photography by Karl Sauer.

Library of Congress Cataloging-in-Publication Data

Names: Sauer, Janet Story, author. | Rossetti, Zachary, author.
Title: Affirming disability : strengths-based portraits of culturally diverse families / Janet Story Sauer, Zachary Rossetti.
Description: New York, NY : Teachers College Press, 2020. | Series: Disability, culture, and equity series | Includes bibliographical references and index.
Identifiers: LCCN 2019036740 (print) | LCCN 2019036741 (ebook) |
    ISBN 9780807763292 (paperback) | ISBN 9780807763308 (hardcover) |
    ISBN 9780807778203 (ebook)
Subjects: LCSH: Children with disabilities—Education—United States. | Immigrant children—Education—United States. | Special education—Social aspects—United States. | Inclusive educatin—Social aspects—United States.
Classification: LCC LC4015 .S24 2020 (print) | LCC LC4015 (ebook) | DDC 371.9—dc23
LC record available at https://lccn.loc.gov/2019036740
LC ebook record available at https://lccn.loc.gov/2019036741

ISBN 978-0-8077-6329-2 (paper)
ISBN 978-0-8077-6330-8 (hardcover)
ISBN 978-0-8077-7820-3 (ebook)

Printed on acid-free paper
Manufactured in the United States of America

To Paula Payne,
Whose selflessness, fierce advocacy, determined leadership, and grace
under pressure resulted in unconditional love, inclusion, and a full and
meaningful life for her son Todd.

To Todd Rossetti,
Who was smarter than most people realized, a loving son and brother, and
lucky to have had a mother like Paula.

Their examples honor the families in this book.

Contents

Foreword

I join authors Sauer and Rossetti as a college educator who cares deeply about preparing teachers to effectively educate the students with disabilities of today, who come from all kinds of backgrounds, in partnership with their diverse families. Many of these families are immigrants, speak different home language(s), and are described broadly as culturally and linguistically diverse. Just like the families in this textbook, I am an immigrant: an able-bodied, Portuguese-American woman who came from the Azores, where I was educated as a teacher and taught for a year before coming to and settling in Massachusetts in the late 1960s.

Much like my colleagues, I have many years of experience in special education for immigrant and other marginalized groups of students with disabilities from early childhood to the doctorate level, in diverse communities in the United States, Brazil, Azores Islands, Cabo Verde, Madeira Islands, and Continental Portugal. Unlike the authors, I had to face language barriers and cultural adaptation to a new community environment as an immigrant to the United States. These experiences contributed to my sensitivity to linguistic and cultural factors as I became a bilingual/English learner/special education public school teacher before becoming a special education professor at a Boston-area university.

As a professor for over 3 decades who has lived the experience of being an immigrant, I share the authors' passion in their commitment to eliminate special education inequities for immigrant families and their children with disabilities through preservice and inservice teacher education. Moreover, I share and applaud the book's emphasis on the change from a deficit approach to a strengths-based vision for transforming special education here and now and beyond.

In *Affirming Disability: Strengths-Based Portraits of Culturally Diverse Families,* professors Sauer and Rossetti break ground in writing an extraordinary textbook that fills a gap in the field of education. The book is geared toward the preparation of current preservice and inservice teachers, who need "to address the learning needs of all students, including immigrants, migrants, special education students, and those from historically underserved groups" (Darling-Hammond & Burns, 2017, p. 186). Most teachers in our American educational settings continue to be monolingual and "White," and many of their students are multilingual and from diverse linguistic, cultural, and racial backgrounds.

To address the inequities associated with the mismatch between students' diversity and their teachers' cultural and linguistic backgrounds, this textbook provides a very well-conceptualized, nonhierarchical, research-based learning solution that is inspirational and action oriented. This textbook reads more like an engaging novel in promoting empathy for equity in general and special education for CLD families.

Indeed, this book goes far beyond the case study approach that is used, for example, by Harry, Klingner, Cramer, and Sturges (2007). It is a culturally responsive text that gives voice to the families. It takes advantage of "portrait narratives," a much more holistic method where the six immigrant families candidly tell in their own words ("na primeira pessoa" in my native Portuguese) about the challenging experiences and inequities they face when navigating the special education system in the United States. These families, from six different cultures, express their experiences within their social, cultural, and educational contexts reflecting what, at times, is sad to recognize. Given the change in demographics that has resulted in an increase in the bilingual ELL population with and without disabilities, educators at all levels, more than ever, need to be better prepared to understand the lives of diverse bilingual English learners with disabilities and their immigrant parents.

At the end of this book, the authors invite the readers to create personal action plans to support CLD families within their local school contexts, particularly during the special education process, where cultural differences and teacher misconception can cause a lot of unnecessary suffering. Readers should get ready to adopt a strengths-based approach to special education and to affirm (dis)ability in culturally and linguistically responsive ways of knowing because, "it is not possible to be family centered without being culturally responsive" (Fults & Harry, 2012, p. 28). I offer my appreciation and congratulations to the authors for creating a long-overdue textbook that proactively contributes to preparing teacher candidates to know more about and better understand the diverse students they will teach.

—Maria de Lourdes B. Serpa, EdD
Professor Emerita of Bilingual EL Special Education
November 11, 2019

REFERENCES

Darling-Hammond, L., & Burns, D. (2017). *Empowered educators: How high-performing systems shape teaching quality around the world*. San Francisco, CA: Jossey-Bass.

Fults, R. M., & Harry, B. (2012). Combining family centeredness and diversity in early childhood teacher training programs. *Teacher Education and Special Education, 35*(1), 27–48. doi.org/10.1177/0888406411399784

Harry, B., Klingner, J. K., Cramer, E. P., & Sturges, K. M. (2007). *Case studies of minority student placement in special education*. New York, NY: Teachers College Press.

Acknowledgments

This book would not have been possible without the support of families, both our own and those with whom we collaborated on these portraits. We are indebted to them all and hope this project can help build greater understanding, respect, and humility in the process of collaborating for educating young people with disabilities, especially children of color involved in the special education process. The emotional work of retelling their experiences, some of which were upsetting, cannot be left unrecognized. We would especially like to thank the reviewers for their valuable suggestions, our colleagues for their support, and our students for continually challenging us to live up to their expectations.

We want to thank Roxanne Hoke-Chandler, whose commitment to supporting families of color with children with disabilities was instrumental to the research and teaching that led to this book. We appreciate the many students who made contributions to our project: From Lesley University, Eman ElGabri, Samantha Hassett, Kit Keown, Aurora La Veglia, and Kasey Salvatore; and from Boston University, Lola Argiro, Oscar Hughes, and Javier Rivera.

CHAPTER 1

Forging Connections in Family Engagement

How might we help to create school cultures from early childhood classrooms through graduate school training that forge the connections between
excellence and equity?

—Sara Lawrence-Lightfoot, 2017

Speaking to a large audience of educators, researchers, activists, and "those who
sit on the boundary lines between these domains," sociologist Sara Lawrence-
Lightfoot (2017) described how we are living in "perilous times." Lawrence-
Lightfoot's lifework has focused on educational ecology—the relational networks
of schools—and while documenting social inequities, she strives to find *goodness*
within the stories. We (Janet and Zach) sat in that audience listening to Lawrence-
Lightfoot beautifully weave the stories of young people from her own decades of
research into the American Educational Research Association (AERA) distinguished lecture at the 2017 AERA conference in San Antonio, TX. She challenged
us "to respond to our feelings of helplessness" and turn our attention to caring for
the young people in our charge. As is her nature, she suggested, "Rather than being
consumed by the darkness, pivot towards the light."

In this book, we hope to give readers knowledge and insights useful for taking
action. Lawrence-Lightfoot says this is "a time when educational cultures need to
reflect the plurality of voices, stories, and cultural narratives; a variety of intelli-
gences and identities; and a spirit of inquiry, criticism, and adventure." In this spirit of critical qualitative research (Denzin, 2017), we offer this contribution to the
body of knowledge about family–school partnerships. We have decades of experience working in pre-K–12 schools, in universities, and in communities around
the country and abroad, with a focus on building relationships with children with
disabilities and their families. We noticed that the plurality of cultural narratives
were largely absent from the research, and set out on our own adventure to document some of these stories.

STRUCTURE AND GOALS OF THE BOOK

In this book, we present six "portrait narratives" (Lawrence-Lightfoot, 2005) of culturally and linguistically diverse (CLD) families of children with disabilities, focusing on their experiences within their social, cultural, and educational contexts. All are immigrant families, and all are led by mothers who are fierce advocates for their children. We document experiences reflecting biases and marginalization that may be frustrating to read and that, on many occasions, were upsetting for the families to retell, but our intention is that our readers (hereafter referred to as "you") will acknowledge these inequities and turn your energy into action that can bring forth positive change. We seek accomplices in our pursuit of creating equitable school cultures of excellence. Toward this end, we put forth three interrelated goals with this book:

1. That school professionals develop nuanced and dynamic understanding of and appreciation for the lives and assets of culturally diverse families of children with disabilities in order to transcend stereotypes of static demographic markers
2. That school professionals reframe disability, shifting from a deficit orientation and/or categorical approach to a strengths-based and individualized understanding of students' strengths, needs, and interests
3. That researchers and school professionals disrupt traditional hierarchies (e.g., the researcher and the researched; school professionals and parents) by collaborating in research and recognizing and learning from the expertise of CLD parents and families.

In each of the six portrait narratives, readers will learn from the experiences of individual families from a variety of cultural backgrounds who navigated the American special education system. It has become an expectation for educators to develop culturally responsive teaching practices in which families' cultural references are used to support children's learning (Ladson-Billings, 1994). But how do teachers learn about families' cultural backgrounds? The practice of "cultural brokering"[1]—the act of bridging between groups or persons of different cultural backgrounds (Jezewski, 1990; Jezewski & Sotnik, 2001)—is something we have found useful for teachers, as well as researchers. In the first portrait, Susan Ou, a Chinese cultural outreach broker, who is also the mother of two boys provided with special education services, asks service providers to "do some research" before working with families—to learn about families and their cultural backgrounds. To support this approach, we begin each portrait with a general introduction to the family's cultural background based on research we did when getting to know the families, including information about their home countries provided by the families, cultural brokers, or others with extensive cultural knowledge. We invite you to join us in this research process by reading these portrait narratives, pausing to reflect on comments by our students interspersed therein—what we call "Student Reflections"—and discussing with classmates and colleagues your considerations and answers to the Reflection Questions at the end of each chapter. We hope you will learn from our qualitative research project that spanned over 5 years and continue your own professional development in understanding the complexities involved in our shared work to improve outcomes for children and youth with disabilities, thus making our school cultures and communities more equitable.

The university students and educational professionals with whom we work as professors in institutions of higher education (IHEs) increasingly recognize the social injustices in society, and they frequently ask for opportunities to learn about ways to "make a difference." We have found, however, that some do not understand our role in contributing to the systemic inequities in schools. Even those of us who think of ourselves as "enlightened professionals" and those in preservice programs preparing to work alongside CLD families may inadvertently contribute to the problematic ways schools in general, and special education systems in particular, discriminate against minority students. For those of us who think we have developed an understanding of these structural issues, we think these family portrait narratives provide additional opportunities to check in with ourselves in order to develop a greater depth of understanding of CLD families and the skills needed to build socially just and inclusive educational communities.

The three goals outlined above rely upon a large and interconnected body of literature. To address the first goal, that school professionals transcend stereotypical and static understandings of CLD families, we draw upon the established work of multicultural education for social justice, then move toward culturally responsive teaching and sustaining practices and the more recent approach of cultural humility. We combine this with family systems research that further reorients school professionals toward approaches in which families are viewed from a perspective that acknowledges their particular cultures, values their ways of knowing their children, and recognizes the complexity of the family unit, especially when disability is involved. To address the second goal, that school professionals reframe disability from a deficit orientation to a strengths-based approach, we draw upon the Disability Studies in Education (DSE) theoretical framework. Included in this is the theoretical framework of Dis/ability Critical Race Studies (DisCrit), which addresses the social construction of both race and disability. This is especially important in a society that is both racist and ableist and perpetuates a deficit approach toward culturally diverse families and individuals with disabilities. To address the third goal of disrupting traditional power imbalances inherent in the research process itself, we use Lawrence-Lightfoot and Davis's (1997) portraiture methodology. Using portraiture allowed us to co-construct each family's story and also share the family stories in a more holistic and creative way than traditional case study reports.

DEVELOPING CULTURAL HUMILITY TO FOSTER FAMILY ENGAGEMENT

Student teachers and practitioners working in schools often face challenges living up to their values of inclusive education and working toward social justice in public schools. In the case of Meagan (Rossetti, Sauer, Bui, & Ou, 2017), an undergraduate preservice teacher (PST) was troubled by the very different ways in which two immigrant families were treated during their children's school meetings. She attended the meetings as an observer, one immediately after the other at two different urban public schools. Both families were Chinese and their children were being discussed in terms of special education. In one meeting Megan witnessed what she described as respectful, meaningful discussions, but in the other meeting she was upset by clearly problematic interactions (e.g., predetermined goals, lack of language interpreter) by the school professionals. After sharing her experiences with her professor, they discussed how as a future teacher she might become effective in facilitating meetings—and communicating between meetings—with families, particularly when there are cultural and linguistic differences between the teacher and the family. Like other university students, Meagan desired more from her coursework than a cursory review of the importance of diversity and culturally responsive practices; she wanted authentic opportunities to learn more about CLD families and methods for developing collaborative partnerships with CLD families during the special education process.

A veteran teacher in English as a second language (ESL), Anastasia recently moved and then joined the faculty of a small school district about an hour's drive from a large city. In her new school, she found that many of the English language learners (ELLs) whose families had recently emigrated from Brazil had been placed in restrictive special education classrooms and were being served by teachers unlicensed in ESL and unfamiliar with the families' Portuguese language and Brazilian culture. Anastasia expressed frustration to us as colleagues in the field and asked about resources and the possibility of collaborating on an action research project about working with the teachers and students' families. In another example, John is a graduate student studying special education. He described feeling overwhelmed as a monolingual White male assigned to a field placement working in a school where over a dozen languages are spoken. He explained how he had searched the Internet to try to learn more about the histories and cultural understandings of his students and their families. John sought out personal and professional resources that might help him communicate with them about the special education process.

Meagan, Anastasia, and John expressed a commitment to working for social justice. They all recognized the need to learn more about the intersection of disability, culture, and language in order to work toward greater educational equity. This book is written to address the needs of preservice professionals and practitioners like Meghan, Anastasia, and John who work with culturally diverse children with disabilities and their families. By reading any or all of these portraits of CLD families, educational professionals will be able to build greater understanding of and empathy for their students and families. Readers are encouraged to appreciate families' assets by taking a strengths-based approach and to practice the reflective process necessary for developing meaningful relationships. Following the portrait chapters, in Chapter 8 readers will be directed to create personal action plans in order to be deliberate and strategic in their efforts to support CLD families within their local school contexts, particularly during the special education process.

Family engagement in special education has been federally mandated for 40 years, since Public Law 94-142 was passed in 1975 and later reauthorized as the Individuals with Disabilities Education Improvement Act (2004), commonly known as IDEA. In fact, IDEA 2004 emphasized family engagement in their children's education as a critical element in improving the effectiveness of special education programs (Turnbull, Turnbull, Erwin, Soodak, & Shogren, 2011). Indeed, family engagement is related to positive student outcomes in special education (Newman, 2004; Ryndak, Alper, Hughes, & McDonnell, 2012). However, many families have indicated a lack of collaboration during the process of determining eligibility for special education and annual Individualized Education Program (IEP) meetings, and have frequently felt that they must adopt a posture of fighting for services for their children (Blackwell & Rossetti, 2014; Resch et al., 2010; Wolfe & Duran, 2013).

These difficulties interacting with professionals in the special education system can be even more prevalent for CLD families due to systemic barriers (Fults & Harry, 2012; Harry, 2008; Olivos, Gallagher, & Aguilar, 2010). In studies of IEP participation, CLD families attended most meetings but were not provided opportunities to contribute, and compared to White and English-speaking families, CLD families reported lower rates of satisfaction in IEP and transition meetings (Blackwell & Rossetti, 2014; Wagner, Newman, Cameto, Javitz, & Valdes, 2012). The lack of collaborative partnerships between CLD families and school professionals is commonly attributed to ethnocentric assumptions about CLD families by teachers from majority cultural backgrounds (Harry, 2008; Wolfe & Duran, 2013). However, we know that many teachers understand the importance of CLD family engagement in their children's educational programs (Trainor, 2010). Effective collaboration is complex, challenging work; thus, there is a need for additional—and ongoing—professional development and support for preservice and inservice professionals to do so.

Education professionals still do not regularly collaborate with CLD families despite years of legislative calls for, and professional training in, increasing family engagement with those who have children labeled as having disabilities (Harry, 2008; Nevin, Smith, & McNeil, 2008; Olivos et al., 2010; Trent, Kea, & Oh, 2008). *Teaching for Diversity and Social Justice* (Adams & Bell, 2016) was first published in 1997 as a primary resource for education personnel preparation. The latest edition added a chapter addressing systemic oppression of people with disabilities that describes compounding issues resulting from interactions between racism and ableism in K–12 education and the need for "cultural shifts toward truly valuing and centering people with diverse minds and bodies" (Ostiguy, Peters, &

Shlasko, 2016, p. 320). In her review of the literature concerning CLD families, Harry (2008) concludes:

> Barriers to the implementation of ideal practices include deficit views of CLD families, cross-cultural misunderstandings related to the meaning of disability, differential values in setting goals for individuals with disabilities, and culturally based differences in caregivers' views of their roles. (p. 372)

Harry (2008) recommends a fundamental shift in teacher preparation to address these barriers. She suggests that "preparation and practice in the actual communication process" with CLD families is needed along with developing critical perspectives. This issue becomes particularly salient considering the increasingly diverse population in the United States, but also in a global society where migration and diaspora are ever more present. As Fults and Harry (2012) explain, "In a multicultural world, it is not possible to be family centered without being culturally responsive" (p. 28). Our students were offered these opportunities in our courses, with multiple guest presentations by CLD mothers of children with disabilities, but we were also cognizant that this approach added the responsibility of teaching others how to be culturally responsive on top of their busy lives and parenting responsibilities. This book resulted from our collective efforts to document and share their stories in a more sustainable approach.

Research has indicated that White, middle-class preservice teachers (PSTs) in teacher preparation programs often hold stereotypical views of urban schools and diverse students that limit their ability to provide effective learning experiences (Cho & DeCastro-Ambrosetti, 2006; Hill, Friedland, & Phelps, 2012). For example, PSTs tend to view low-income learners and students of color as having "disadvantaged" home environments that make them more difficult to teach (McDiarmid & Price, 1990; Pang & Sablan, 1998). PSTs have reported less interest in becoming teachers of urban minority children (Groulx, 2001) and tend to possess low expectations for urban students (Terrill & Mark, 2000), students of color (Gay, 2010), and English language learners (Rodriguez, Manner, & Darcy, 2010).

PSTs' lack of capacity and their unwillingness to change complicates efforts to develop multicultural thinking and sociocultural awareness (Clift & Brady, 2005). In addition, PSTs tend to think superficially about their attitudes and beliefs about diversity, and some may even resent and/or resist consideration of multicultural principles (Gay, 2010). Much of what they bring to a teacher preparation context is grounded in personal beliefs, developed during their own history as learners, about what teaching should be and how students should behave (Barnes, 2000; Kagan, 1992). Strategies intended to mitigate stereotypical perspectives, such as coursework or urban field experiences, may in some cases reinforce deficit-oriented preconceived notions of diverse learners (Hyland & Noffke, 2005), especially if the experience fails to provide guidance and critical reflection (Tiezzi & Cross, 1997).

In his article about the need for systems change in teacher education, Haddix (2017) explains the challenges for preparing teachers with "the cultural capital and racial and linguistic backgrounds to teach the current diverse student population." Writing as a person of color, he points out, "Regardless of background, teachers struggle to comprehend and employ culturally responsive practice" (p. 144). That cultural understanding is not limited to one group identity is noteworthy, and helps with understanding the distinction between cultural competence and *cultural humility*. The lifelong practice of developing cultural humility has been a focus within social work and education (Hook et al., 2013). Lund and Lee (2015) describe their service learning research project for preservice teachers working with immigrant families as a valuable way to develop cultural humility. The idea of developing cultural humility demonstrates that it is not just a collection of information, but a change in mindset and an approach to working with people, in this case with CLD families, as an ongoing process involving a change of attitudes.

Disproportionality in special education is widely reported and understood as a complex social, cultural, and political interaction (Connor, Ferri, & Annamma, 2016; Skiba, Artiles, Kozleski, Losen, & Harry, 2016; Sullivan & Bal, 2013). This overrepresentation phenomenon has been attributed in part to school professionals' lack of experience with and understanding of families from cultural and/or linguistic minority groups (Howard, 2010). In 2010 almost half of the public school student population consisted of persons of color (Feistritzer, 2011), and 21% spoke a language other than English (U.S. Department of Education, 2012), yet their teachers were, and continue to be, predominantly White, female, monolingual, and middle-class (Barnes, 2006; Galman, Pica-Smith, & Rosenberger, 2010; Green et al., 2011; Haddix, 2017). Such an acknowledgment of differences between students and their teachers is indisputably important; equally important is the understanding of the difference with regard to dis/ability markers within families and how this plays a part in the American special education structure. For instance, in their review of special education in Massachusetts, Hehir, Grindal, and Eidelman (2012) found "an uneven picture of special education policy and practice" (p. 2) where low-income students and students of color were disproportionately served in more restrictive settings and that these placements may have contributed to their lower performance on standardized tests.

Unfortunately, many introductory courses in preservice professional programs and graduate programs for inservice teachers and related service providers reify the marginalized status of people with disabilities and their families. In an effort to disrupt this imbalance, some universities have employed strategies such as reading autobiographies authored by people with disabilities, watching videos of families, and inviting family members as guests to talk about their experiences. While we embrace all of these approaches, the availability of these human and material resources can be very limited, and sometimes the resources themselves perpetuate stereotypes and a deficit orientation. Recently, there has been an increase in the number of autobiographies and family memoirs about families of children with disabilities; however, these are primarily authored by highly educated White professionals with social, economic, and cultural privileges (Ferguson, Hanreddy, & Ferguson, 2013; Sauer & Ferguson, 2013). The few research-based case studies are limited and/or formal in their academic discourse (e.g., Steeley & Lukacs, 2015). Videos tend to be similarly limited, and they rely upon a family's full disclosure. Due to cultural, social, economic, and sometimes logistical circumstances, it can be difficult to identify CLD families to come into the university setting to share their experiences with college students (Sauer & Kasa, 2012). Moreover, researchers working to document the experiences of CLD families can be constrained by their own "otherness," and some of the families report they fear retribution or possibly deportation should they allow their stories to be published (Francis, Gross, & Casarez-Velazquez, 2016; Rossetti, Burke, & Sauer, 2016).

These limitations and the complex power dynamics involved with bringing these CLD families to print need to be acknowledged. We are grateful to the many families who have volunteered their time over the years to talk with our students or co-present with us at special education conferences for inservice professionals. Discriminatory practices against students of color who are labeled with disabilities are well documented. In his *Brown Lecture*, Professor Alfredo Artiles (2017) argued for the possibility and promise of equity research in which educational researchers would not repeat the injustices experienced in society, particularly against children and youth of color involved in special education. He emphasized the importance of intersectional spaces in which students are members of both disability and other marked identity categories. Artiles recounted the story of Kanita, a 1st-grader in Florida, and her social ecology that was detailed in Harry and Klingner's (2014) ethnographic study. Artiles pointed out how the interpretations of Kanita by the various educational professionals were largely influenced by their historically limited or static understanding of the child's context and her family's cultural norms. Harry and Klingner used their cultural knowledge and research tools to document an alternative dynamic, positive interpretation of the child grounded in the family's perspective. They concluded in their follow-up to their original study, "Ten years after the termination of this study, the federal view of special education services has changed little . . . we urge caution and careful consideration of cultural and linguistic diversity when making eligibility determination" (Harry & Klingner, 2014, pp. 183–184). It is troubling to state that our longitudinal study of culturally diverse families found that many of these issues persist.

THEORETICAL FRAMEWORK—DISABILITY STUDIES IN EDUCATION

We teach from a Disability Studies in Education (DSE) theoretical framework that privileges the voices and experiences of people labeled with disabilities to counter ableist narratives and the tendency for people without disabilities to talk about and for them. Disability Studies (DS) emphasizes that disability does not reside in individuals, but rather is socially constructed in specific sociocultural contexts (Baglieri, Valle, Connor, & Gallagher, 2011). DSE applies the DS perspective to public education, aiming to reframe how school professionals view students with disabilities and to reform the special education system (Gabel, 2005). We see this combination as contributing to a greater understanding of human diversity and the work toward social justice. DSE provides a necessary critical approach to "investigate the construction of disability, language, and culture in the context of meritocratic systems that create, mask and perpetuate inequalities related to . . . stratifying categories" (Disability Studies in Education Special Interest Group, 2017). Giroux (2010) contends that there is a need for "understanding pedagogy as a deeply civic, political and moral practice—that is, pedagogy as a practice for freedom" (p. 715). Critical pedagogy along with Disability Studies in Education offer an alternative approach to thinking about the relationships between people with disabilities—and their families—and those hired to support them (Bogdan & Taylor, 1992; Brantlinger, Klingner, Richardson, & Taylor, 2005; Giroux, 2010; Nevin et al., 2008).

In her comparative analysis of American and Italian efforts to develop inclusive education, DS scholar Beth Ferri (2015) writes that in spite of laws intended to bring greater equity to children with disabilities, "We have yet to fully change the dynamic of that classroom, which created the problem of disability in the first place" (p. 15). She explains how the dualistic general/special education structures were established prior to the development of the DSE framework, and suggests that a DSE framework is needed to bring about the underlying transformation of schools in which teachers "would both expect and embrace diversity and difference" (p. 19) and incorporate disability within the curriculum, rather than thinking of it as existing within individual children. Although the International Classification of Functioning, Disability, and Health "allows one to view disability as a dynamic interaction between the person and the environment, . . . prevailing definitions of disability used by Federal agencies do not reflect the new paradigm of disability concepts because the Federal definitions typically stress limitations" (U.S. Department of Education, February 15, 2006, p. 8171).

Reframing disability in this way requires that school professionals practice strengths-based approaches to working with culturally and linguistically diverse families of children with disabilities to replace dated deficit models that emphasize supposed limitations of both families and their children. Strengths-based approaches to teaching children who are learning English is well established in literacy research (Moll, Amanti, Neff, & Gonzalez, 1992). Moll et al.'s (1992) "funds of knowledge" provides the basis for Pacheco and Gutiérrez's (2009) cultural–historical theoretical approach to literacy and learning. DSE builds on this strengths-based and culturally situated approach through its emphasis on presuming competence (Biklen & Burke, 2006) and understanding intersectionality (Cosier & Ashby, 2016). The portraits in this book reflect a growing recognition of the sociocultural dynamic as an integral part of negotiated meanings of disability and its relationship with CLD families' lived experiences.

Regarding CLD families' engagement in the special education process, we utilize the DisCrit theoretical framework and Yosso's (2005) community cultural wealth framework. *DisCrit* refers to Dis/ability Critical Race Studies, which combines aspects of critical race theory (CRT) and Disability Studies (DS) to engage in a dual analysis of race and ability (Annamma, Connor, & Ferri, 2013). DisCrit's first tenet stresses that "the forces of racism and ableism circulate interdependently, often in neutralized and invisible ways, to uphold notions of normalcy" (Annamma et al., 2013, p. 11). Yosso's (2005) community cultural wealth framework, also rooted in CRT, problematizes the persistent ethnocentric assumption that CLD families are unable and uninterested in participating in their children's education. To the contrary, CLD families face systemic barriers limiting the extent to which their multiple forms of capital are recognized by dominant societal groups (e.g., White education professionals), often leading to disempowerment (Harry, 2008; Wolfe & Duran, 2013). Rather than understand and value the capital families have, school personnel emphasize their own technical special education knowledge, which many immigrant families do not initially have (Trainor, 2010). Further, many parents of children with disabilities rely on social capital via relationships with other parents of children with disabilities (Solomon, Pistrang, & Barker, 2001). Yet such networks often exclude CLD families (Harry, 2002).

Together, these frameworks recognize that in a society that values Whiteness and ability as cultural norms, differences from these norms will be viewed as deficits. DSE challenges the oppressive nature of special educational systems that inequitably educate students with multidimensional identities. Thus these portraits of CLD families involved with special education serve to reframe school perceptions from those that marginalize families to those that affirm and value their contextually situated lives.

Using a DSE theoretical framework, this book seeks to provide university students with meaningful opportunities to learn directly from CLD families while preparing to become skilled active "listeners" (or readers) who can more critically understand the complexities they witness in the field rather than inadvertently contribute toward reifying inequities (Harry, 2008). Rather than acculturating preservice practitioners into the role of experts who diagnose and remediate children with disabilities, and who may make assumptions about CLD families' motives regarding their involvement in their children's education, DSE provides a different paradigm in which families are viewed as partners in the collaborative process of designing holistic support systems that recognize the complexities and humanity of individuals with disabilities and their families (Annamma et al., 2013; Sauer & Ferguson, 2013).

METHODOLOGY—STRENGTHS-BASED PORTRAITURE

The third goal involves disrupting traditional hierarchies of power. Power imbalance is evident both in the structural organization of schooling and in the research process used to study education systems. Addressing the needs of America's children and their families is a complex process that needs greater scrutiny if we are to disrupt the cycle of practices, often based on traditional research approaches that perpetuate inequality in schools. It is a work in progress, and one that requires many opportunities for educational professionals and researchers to construct cultural humility and develop culturally sustaining pedagogies and methodologies. In our own professional lives, we recognize the need for continual professional development in these areas, as you will see in this section where we describe our own positionalities and some of our own limitations in the process of researching and writing this book. We acknowledge how important it is to persist with the work of our own (re)developing self-awareness, or critical reflection, if we are to model the skills we expect our students to develop (Ferri, 2015). We are frequently challenged by our students, colleagues, and the CLD families with whom we work to critically reflect and find ways within our own spheres of activism[2] to work toward social justice.

Positionality

Recognizing that qualitative researchers are the analytic tools in their work, we need to position ourselves in relation to the focus of our project and describe how our experiences inform it (Creswell, 2013).

Janet Sauer identifies as a White, cisgender, middle-class, able-bodied, English-speaking woman raised in a large Catholic family in the Midwest. I (Janet) worked in pre-K–12 schools in Africa and in the United States on the Navajo Reservation and in Ohio, Iowa, Colorado, and Boston. I teach preservice teachers in a medium-sized private college in the Northeast where I participate regularly in the university diversity-sponsored events and workshops about topics such as white privilege and Black Lives Matter. In one of these workshops, I joined colleagues from varied disciplines in a 2-year study group that emerged from one of the annual week-long Cultural Literacy Curriculum Institutes. The study group morphed into a writing group that resulted in the book *Culturally Responsive Teaching and Reflection in Higher Education* (Cochrane, Chhabra, Jones, & Spragg, 2017), which includes essays about self-awareness, pedagogy and power, and community practice. The colleagues developed relationships in which they continue to call one another out (or "in" to discuss) when they witness instances in which faculty or the institution does not fulfill claims of equity and inclusion.

Zach Rossetti identifies as a White, cisgender, middle-class, temporarily able-bodied, monolingual English-speaking man raised in a large Catholic family in the Northeast. I (Zach) worked in public, independent, and residential schools as a special educator, inclusion facilitator, and dorm parent. Currently, I am an associate professor of special education at a private research university in the Northeast. My research examines family engagement in special education, friendships between students with and without disabilities, and sibling roles and relationships.

My work was and is motivated by my late brother, Todd Christopher Rossetti (January 17, 1980–April 5, 2019). Todd was a huge Boston Red Sox and Boston

Bruins fan, loved chocolate cake, and was very social. That he was so outgoing is even more impressive because he did not speak, used a wheelchair, and needed support throughout his day due to his cerebral palsy. Communicating and connecting with others without speaking was one of many lessons he taught me. We spent countless hours together laughing, watching Red Sox games (on TV and at Fenway Park), sometimes arguing or getting annoyed with each other, and mostly just hanging out together.

I learned early on that others did not always view Todd as I did. When I was younger, I noticed others staring at him when we were in a public space (grocery store, amusement park, hockey rink). I remember wondering why he was not invited to birthday parties when he was in school and why so many adults (teachers especially) spoke in a childish, singsong voice to him, even as a teenager and young adult with facial hair! When I was older, I attended a couple of IEP meetings with our mother, experiencing what it felt like to be outnumbered and finally understanding why she described that she had to fight with the school to get Todd what he needed. Until then, I assumed others would get to know Todd and treat him as we did in our family. The reality included low expectations and surface-level greetings rather than rigorous academics and authentic relationships. Too many people missed out on the privilege of truly knowing Todd.

Co-Construction

Keeping in mind Lawrence-Lightfoot's (2005) cautionary words to researchers who might unwittingly reify the power imbalances evident among school personnel and families, we have sought to share in this book both the *content* of knowledge that the families with whom we worked have, as well as the *process* by which we collaborated. We think the extensive *content* of information and insights from the families is obvious in the portraits, but the *process* by which sentences were written and words and images chosen may not be as self-evident to the readers. The process by which we worked with each family was unique, yet all of the family portraits were approached as a form of co-construction. We conceptualized the book alongside some of the families while we discussed the need for something other than formulaic summaries of case studies that we thought would be too constraining.

Horner (2016) provides a useful explanation of the meaning of *co-constructed research*: "I have increasingly started to view co-construction as an ethic and aspiration rather than (or more than) a field or methodology" (p. 8). She continues, "Co-constructed research is research that facilitates the co-construction of knowledge at its core. Here the organising ethic is the equal partnership between academics and partners" (p. 8). We would like to acknowledge how the process of co-construction was different for each family portrait; the various factors depended upon a particular family's time they had to dedicate themselves to the writing process, their personal preferences, and confidence with regard to writing in English (most of these parents—all mothers—had attended institutions of higher education). Oanh and Tiny's family portrait, for instance, evolved over nearly five years of developing a relationship with dozens of exchanges in multiple contexts (e.g., in university classrooms, at special education conferences, over coffee, and through phone calls and email exchanges). Some were formal and some informal. A specific and formal example involved us asking a parent to read the transcript of interviews we had recorded and transcribed, to see what she might have wanted to change to more accurately reflect what she intended to express (i.e., first-level member checking). Other examples involved showing the parents our students' assignments (mini-portraits of the families, response poetry, personal reflections) written after hearing them share their stories in a class, and having a conversation about how students interpreted particular aspects of the story. Such feedback often made its way into a family's portrait, while also informing future data collection in the ongoing nature of the project.

In our effort to disrupt the researcher–researched power dynamic endemic in the process of writing these stories, the family portraits in this book utilize methods of qualitative research in which participants became co-researchers (e.g., Berger & Feucht, 2012; Biklen & Burke, 2006; Sauer, 2012); in particular, CLD family members contributed to the editing and retelling of their stories. For instance, after reading one of our students' papers, a parent asked if it wasn't "fairy-tale sounding"? She, like Disability Studies scholars, became concerned when some people think of individuals with disabilities, and sometimes their families, as heroic; these parents are not seeking accolades or pity; they seek *understanding* of their complex, and ordinary, lives (Shapiro, 1993). They caution readers not to think of their stories as token cultural representatives. In some cases, we have co-authored parts of this book with families and our students, and in all chapters we include direct quotes from family members.

Participants

The participants (see Table 1.1) in the research study who are featured in this book represent six immigrant families of children with disabilities. For each family, we

Table 1.1. Participant Demographics

Participant	Portrait	Ethnicity
Susan	Susan, Bruce, and Ian	Chinese immigrant
Oanh	Oanh and Tiny	Vietnamese immigrant
María	María and Juan	Latina immigrant (El Salvador)
Punita	Punita and Sachin	First-generation Indian American; husband is Indian immigrant
Kimiya	Shirin and Samin	Iranian immigrant
Sahra	Sahra and Qalid	Somali refugee

interacted with one participant and co-researcher who were all women; five were mothers and one was a sister of the individuals with disabilities. Each participant (and their families) could be considered culturally and linguistically diverse. We adhered to a broad definition for cultural and linguistic diversity in the United States as "individuals whose primary language is not English and/or who are not European American" (Wolfe & Duran, 2013, p. 5).

These women joined the study through purposeful sampling after (and as) we developed professional and personal relationships with them. This process was individualized for each participant, and it included multiple meetings to build rapport, describe the purpose and procedures in the research project, and schedule data collection. Some participants preferred face-to-face discussions, as email was not an effective means of communication for them, while others opted for email communication. Some participants were bi- or multilingual, utilizing their English proficiency to engage with the monolingual researchers. For others, we benefited from cultural brokers and bilingual graduate students to act as language interpreters and translators of written materials. We (Janet and Zach) certainly recognize our own language limitations (i.e., monolingual English speakers) as one of our shortcomings in this study and our ongoing work.

Data Collection

Data were collected during the past 5 years. Again, this process was individualized for each participant due to the timing of when they joined the project (i.e., some joined sooner than others) and practical factors such as the families' time and willingness to disclose personal information. For example, Oanh's portrait is the most exemplary in terms of depth due to an abundance of rich data because she was one of the first to join the project, comfortable presenting to audiences, and proficient in written English. We sought similar results with the other participants, but encountered some limitations with the mothers' availability, English proficiency, and various situational factors. It was difficult for one mother to write in English, and she was unable to meet for interviews and conversations due to her busy schedule (e.g., work, childcare). Another mother dropped out of the project at the suggestion of her lawyer because she was engaged in the dispute resolution process, specifically mediation, regarding her child's proposed Individualized Education Program.

Data were collected several ways. Class presentations included visits to university classes where the participants shared their stories, along with photographs and related artifacts including visual supports and their children's Individualized Family Service Plan (IFSP) or Individualized Education Program (IEP). Additionally, they participated in formal in-depth interviews, as well as informal interviews and ongoing conversations at community settings with the authors (e.g., before or after presentation at a university class, at conferences and other community cultural events). Each class presentation and formal in-depth interview was audio-recorded and transcribed verbatim. The authors also documented the class presentations, formal and informal interviews, and ongoing conversations with detailed field notes and researcher memos highlighting patterns in the data and topics to follow up on in subsequent interviews or conversations.

The data collection also included formal course assignments by over 100 university students after each class presentation. The students were preservice (undergraduate students) or inservice (most of the graduate students) professionals in special education, elementary education, school counseling, and the related services. Specifically, the students created "mini-portraits" of each child based on the mothers' descriptions of their experiences. We designed the mini-portrait assignments to counter the clinical nature of case study reports assigned in prior iterations of our courses and typically used in special education. The traditional case study report usually begins with descriptions of the child's disability diagnosis and related characteristics, and thus is categorical rather than individualized. Additionally, case study reports tend to take a deficit-oriented approach, highlighting the child's challenges and identifying them as innate; they often do not include mention of the child's interests, strengths, familial context, linguistic preferences, or cultural background. Alternately, the mini-portraits foster holistic descriptions of children with disabilities that emphasize who they are, what they can do (i.e., strengths, skills, and interests in addition to their areas of need), what supports they need, and what strategies or approaches work best to provide those individualized supports. The mini-portraits also include the children's familial contexts, linguistic preferences, and cultural backgrounds. The university students were instructed that the mini-portraits could include alternative forms to the traditional reflection paper (e.g., narrative, poem, artwork) based on their interpretation of what was important to the presenter and her child. The mini-portrait assignments also included a reflection section in which university students reacted personally and professionally to the presentation and identified at least two implications for their future practice.

Data Analysis

Data analysis was guided by Ayers's (1989) explanation that linking individual portrait themes to one another and to the "cultural and institutional context" (p. 126) contributes valuable insights to our understanding of complex issues. To develop these individual portrait narratives for this study, the data were analyzed systematically and inductively using constant-comparative procedures (Bogdan & Biklen, 2003; Creswell, 2013) and discourse analysis (Brantlinger, Klingner, Richardson, & Taylor, 2005) of transcripts from the class presentations and in-depth interviews, field notes, and other written documents including IFSPs and IEPs. The researchers engaged in an iterative process with several cycles of analyzing data, discussing with each other and refining analysis, presenting to the participants for their feedback, discussing and refining analysis again, and collecting additional data that would be incorporated into the ongoing analysis.

Portrait Development

Each of the following portraits was co-constructed through an iterative and individualized process by one or both of the authors, the mother featured in the portrait, and university students or colleagues who attended the mothers' presentations, had expertise in a related area, or shared cultural and linguistic backgrounds. The mothers served as experts with valued knowledge through selecting what information they wanted others to know about their experiences. We incorporated mothers' existing writing about their experiences when available. We asked all mothers to contribute new writing, if possible, based on their time, language proficiency, and writing facility, using the following prompt: What are the most important things you want people to know about your experiences? In some instances, additional informal interviews were conducted in an effort to capture more details.

The writing process was, again, individualized for each participant. Oanh, Punita, and Sahra were adamant about authoring their own chapters; Oanh and Punita contributed in written text, while Sahra orally told her story, as is Somali tradition, to a co-author (Amy) of her chapter who transcribed what she said. The authors shaped and revised chapters, incorporated prior written text about or by the families (e.g., for Oanh and Susan), added the Student Reflections (from our students' assignments, which were unidentifiable and treated as research data; all students consented to participate), wrote the reflection questions, and then shared with the participants to review and revise or provide more feedback. Susan and María did not want to author their chapters; thus they conveyed their stories through formal and informal interviews with the first author (Janet) and co-author (Maureen) of their chapters. The chapter about Samin and Shirin was written by their sister/daughter, Kimiya. Kimiya had begun to write about her family in her doctoral dissertation, discussed the purpose of the book with the authors, and elaborated on her family's story after conducting three additional in-depth interviews with her mother, Shirin.

Our procedures included several critical credibility measures for empirical qualitative research (Brantlinger, Jiminez, Klingner, Pugach, & Richardson, 2005). We utilized data triangulation by collecting and analyzing varied data sources in the development of the mini-portrait narratives of CLD families. We also utilized investigator triangulation, as the co-creation of the mini-portrait narratives occurred within an iterative process involving ongoing analysis and feedback between multiple authors as described above. We incorporated second-level member checks through the review of student summaries of class presentations (i.e., the original mini-portrait course assignments) by the presenters (CLD mothers) themselves. Additionally, the mini-portrait narratives include thick, detailed description of the CLD families' experiences and perspectives to support their meaning making and our collective interpretations of all the data.

The resulting family portraits intend to reflect the depth and complexity of these families in ways that honor their knowledge, cultures, and experiences. The authors hope these portraits and our related analyses contribute to the body of qualitative research using portraiture methodology that was first envisioned by Lawrence-Lightfoot and Davis (1997). So, like Ayers (1989), and more recently Catone (2017), who used portraiture to focus on teachers, and similar to Sauer's (2012) portraits of White, Midwestern families of children with disabilities, we sought to bring together the art and the science of qualitative research to embrace "the complexity, dynamics, and subtlety of human experience" (Lawrence-Lightfoot & Davis, 1997, p. xv). Lastly, we fully recognize that we experienced the privilege of time with these mothers and families in a way that teachers, counselors, and therapists do not. Thus, while we share fully developed portraits, we encourage readers to identify aspects that are especially relevant to their situation and to enact the practical strategies to reframe and affirm disability and forge connections with CLD families that are included in Chapter 8.

CONCLUSION

This book addresses what teacher education course texts and professional development materials often lack: a strengths-based approach, informed by cultural humility, to working alongside CLD families with children with disabilities who are often doubly marginalized in their status. We have written this book for our students and colleagues working in school contexts seeking greater social justice. Ultimately, however, we wrote this book for families and their children, who we hope will receive greater equity and respect with regard to their educational experiences.

NOTES

1. The term "cultural outreach broker" was first introduced to us by Oanh Bui, the Vietnamese mother who authored her own portrait narrative in Chapter 3. Bui adopted Jezewski's (1990) definition used in the guide *Bridging the Cultural Divide in Health Care Settings*: "that cultural brokering is the act of bridging, linking, or mediating between groups or persons of different cultural backgrounds for the purpose of reducing conflict or producing change" (National Center for Cultural Competence, 2004, p. vii). For more information, see nccc.georgetown.edu/documents/Cultural_Broker_Guide_English.pdf.

2. The phrase "spheres of influence" has roots in colonialism, and was used to describe the relationship between colonial powers and those under their control. It has since been appropriated in a variety of disciplines to describe situations in which people might make a positive influence on changing systems. We originally used this expression to describe our positionality within Institutions of Higher Educations, but have since adopted the phrase "spheres of activism" (Nixon, 2009) as one we find more fitting.

REFERENCES

Adams, M., & Bell, L. A. (with Goodman, D. J., & Joshi, K. Y.). (Eds.). (2016). *Teaching for diversity and social justice* (3rd ed.). New York, NY: Routledge.

Annamma, S. A., Connor, D., & Ferri, B. (2013). Dis/ability critical race studies (DisCrit): Theorizing at the intersections of race and dis/ability. *Race, Ethnicity, and Education, 16*, 1–31. doi:10.1080/13613324.2012.730511

Artiles, A. (2017, October 19). *Re-envisioning equity research: Disability identification disparities as a case in point.* 14th annual Brown Lecture in Education Research, American Educational Research Association, Washington, DC. Retrieved from youtube.com/watch?v=DtmwoCmPw3s&feature=youtu.be

Ayers, W. (1989). *The good preschool teacher: Six teachers reflect on their lives.* New York, NY: Teachers College Press.

Baglieri, S., Valle, J. W., Connor, D. J., & Gallagher, D. J. (2011). Disability studies in education: The need for a plurality of perspectives on disability. *Remedial and Special Education, 32*, 267–278. doi:10.1177/0741932510362200

Barnes, C. J. (2006). Preparing preservice teachers to teach in a culturally responsive way. *The Negro Educational Review, 57*, 85–100.

Barnes, G. V. (2000). Self-efficacy and teacher effectiveness. *Journal of String Research, 1*, 627–643.

Berger, R. J., & Feucht, J. (2012). "Thank you for your words": Observations from a disability summer camp. *Qualitative Inquiry, 18*, 76–85. doi:10.1177/1077800411426119

Biklen, D., & Burke, J. (2006). Presuming competence. *Equity & Excellence in Education, 39*, 166–175.

Blackwell, W. H., & Rossetti, Z. S. (2014). The development of individualized education programs: Where have we been and where should we go now? *SAGE Open, 4*(2). Retrieved from journals.sagepub.com/doi/10.1177/2158244014530411

Bogdan, R. C., & Biklen, S. K. (2003). *Qualitative research for education: An introduction to theories and methods* (4th ed.). Boston, MA: Allyn & Bacon.

Bogdan, R., & Taylor, S. J. (1992). The social construction of humanness: Relationships with severely disabled people. In P. M. Ferguson, D. L. Ferguson, & S. J. Taylor (Eds.), *Interpreting disability: A qualitative reader* (pp. 275–294). New York, NY: Teachers College Press.

Brantlinger, E., Jiminez, R., Klingner, J., Pugach, M., & Richardson, V. (2005). Qualitative studies in special education. *Exceptional Children, 71*, 195–207. Retrieved from dx.doi.org/10.1177/001440290507100205

Brantlinger, E., Klingner, J., Richardson, V., & Taylor, S. J. (2005). Importance of experimental as well as empirical qualitative studies in special education. *Mental Retardation, 43*, 92–119.

Catone, K. (2017). *The pedagogy of teacher activism: Portraits of four teachers for justice.* New York, NY: Peter Lang.

Cho, G., & DeCastro-Ambrosetti, D. (2006). Is ignorance bliss? Preservice teachers' attitudes toward multicultural education. *The High School Journal, 89*(2), 24–28.

Clift, R. T., & Brady, P. (2005). Research on methods courses and field experiences. In M. Cochran-Smith & K. M. Zeichner (Eds.), *Studying teacher education: The report of the AERA panel on research and teacher education* (pp. 309–424). Washington, DC: AERA.

Cochrane, S. V., Chhabra, M., Jones, M. A., & Spragg, D. (Eds.). (2017). *Culturally responsive teaching and reflection in higher education: Promising practices from the Cultural Literacy Curriculum Institute.* New York, NY: Routledge.

Connor, D. J., Ferri, B. A., & Annamma, S. A. (2016). *DisCrit: Disability studies and critical race theory in education.* New York, NY: Teachers College Press.

Cosier, M., & Ashby, C. (Eds.). (2016). *Enacting change from within: Disability studies meets teaching and teacher education.* New York, NY: Peter Lang.

Creswell, J. W. (2013). *Qualitative inquiry and research design: Choosing among five approaches.* Los Angeles, CA: SAGE

Denzin, N. K. (2017). Critical qualitative inquiry. *Qualitative Inquiry, 23,* 8–16. doi:10.1177/1077800416681864

Disability Studies in Education Special Interest Group. (2017). *Call for proposals.* Retrieved from aera.net/SIG143/Message-from-SIG-Chair

Feistritzer, C. E. (2011). *Profile of Teachers in the U.S. 2011.* Washington, DC: National Center for Education Information.

Ferguson, D. L., Hanreddy, A., & Ferguson, P. M. (2013). Finding a voice: Families' roles in schools. In L. Florian (Ed.), *The Sage handbook on special education: Vol. 2* (2nd edition) (pp.763–783). Thousand Oaks, CA: Sage.

Ferri, B. (2015). Inclusion for the 21st century: Why we need disability studies in education. *Italian Journal of Special Education for Inclusion, 3*(2), 11–22.

Francis, G. L., Gross, J.M.S., & Casarez-Velazquez, K. (2016, December). *Transition experiences of Spanish-speaking families.* Paper presented at the TASH Annual Conference, St. Louis, MO.

Fults, R. M., & Harry, B. (2012). Combining family centeredness and diversity in early childhood teacher training programs. *Teacher Education and Special Education, 35,* 27–48. doi:10.1177/0888406411399784

Gabel, S. L. (Ed.). (2005). *Disability studies in education: Readings in theory and method.* New York, NY: Peter Lang.

Galman, S., Pica-Smith, C., & Rosenberger, C. (2010). Aggressive and tender navigations: Teacher educators confront Whiteness in their practice. *Journal of Teacher Education, 61,* 225–236. doi:10.1177/0022487109359776

Gay, G. (2010). Acting on beliefs in teacher education for cultural diversity. *Journal of Teacher Education, 61,* 143–152. doi:10.177/0022487109347320.

Giroux, H. A. (2010). Rethinking education as the practice of freedom: Paulo Freire and the promise of critical pedagogy. *Truthout, Op-Ed.* Retrieved from truthout.org/articles/rethinking-education-as-the-practice-of-freedom-paulo-freire-and-the-promise-of-critical-pedagogy/

Green, A. M., Kent, A. M., Lewis, J., Feldman, P., Motley, M. R., Baggett, P. V., . . . Simpson, J. (2011). Experiences of elementary preservice teachers in an urban summer enrichment program. *The Western Journal of Black Studies, 35*(4), 227–239.

Groulx, J. G. (2001). Changing preservice teacher perceptions of minority schools. *Urban Education, 36,* 60–92.

Haddix, M. M. (2017). Diversifying teaching and teacher education: Beyond rhetoric and toward real change. *Journal of Literacy Research, 49,* 141–149. doi:10.1177/1086296X16683422

Harry, B. (2002). Trends and issues in serving culturally diverse families of children with disabilities. *The Journal of Special Education, 36,* 131–138. doi:10.1177/00224669020360030301

Harry, B. (2008). Collaboration with culturally and linguistically diverse families: Ideal versus reality. *Exceptional Children, 74,* 372–388.

Harry, B., & Klingner, J. K. (2014). *Why are so many minority students in special education? Understanding race and disability in schools.* New York, NY: Teachers College Press.

Hehir, T., Grindal, T., & Eidelman, H. (2012). *Review of special education in the commonwealth of Massachusetts.* Boston, MA: Massachusetts Department of Elementary and Secondary Education.

Hill, P. D. P., Friedland, E. S., & Phelps, S. (2012). How teacher candidates' perceptions of urban students are influenced by field experiences: A review of the literature. *Action in Teacher Education, 34,* 77–96.

Hook, J. N., Davis, D. E., Owen, J., Worthington, E. L., Jr., & Utsey, S. O. (2013). Cultural humility: Measuring openness to culturally diverse clients. *Journal of Counseling Psychology, 60,* 353–366. doi: 10.1037/a0032595

Horner, L. K. (2016). *Co-constructing research: A critical literature review.* Arts & Humanities Research Council. Retrieved from connected-communities.org/index.php/project_resources/coconstructing-research-a-critical-literature-review

Howard, T. C. (2010). *Why race and culture matter in schools: Closing the achievement gap in America's classrooms.* New York, NY: Teachers College Press.

Hyland, N. E., & Noffke, S. E. (2005). Understanding diversity through social and community inquiry: An action-research study. *Journal of Teacher Education, 56,* 367–381. doi:10.1177/0022487105279568

Jezewski, M. A. (1990). Culture brokering in migrant farm worker health care. *Western Journal of Nursing Research, 12*(4), 497–513.

Jezewski, M. A., & Sotnik, P. (2001). *Culture brokering: Providing culturally competent rehabilitation services to foreign-born persons.* Buffalo, NY: Center for International Rehabilitation Research Information and Exchange (CIRRIE). Retrieved from cirrie-sphhp.webapps.buffalo.edu/culture/monographs/cb.php

Kagan, D. M. (1992). Professional growth among preservice and beginning teachers. *Review of Educational Research, 62,* 129–169. doi:10.3102/00346543062002129

Ladson-Billings, G. (1994). *The dreamkeepers: Successful teachers of African American children.* San Francisco, CA: Jossey-Bass Publishers.

Lawrence-Lightfoot, S. (2005). Reflections on portraiture: A dialogue between art and science. *Qualitative Inquiry, 11,* 3–15. doi:10.1177/1077800404270955

Lawrence-Lightfoot, S. (2017, April 28). *"Let the great brown river smile." Liberating frames and educational discourses: On view, voice, and visibility.* Distinguished Lecture presented at the annual meeting of the American Educational Research Association, San Antonio, Texas. Retrieved from www.youtube.com/watch?v=0qbGoo0N0lU

Lawrence-Lightfoot, S., & Davis, J. H. (1997). *The art and science of portraiture.* San Francisco, CA: Jossey-Bass.

Lund, D. E., & Lee, L. (2015). Fostering cultural humility among pre-service teachers: Connecting with children and youth of immigrant families through service-learning. *Canadian Journal of Education, 38*(2), 1–30.

McDiarmid, G. W., & Price, J. (1990). *Prospective teachers' views of diverse learners: A study of the participants in the ABCD project* (Research Report 90-6). East Lansing: Michigan State University, National Center for Research on Teacher Education.

Moll, L. C., Amanti, C., Neff, D., & Gonzalez, N. (1992). Funds of knowledge for teaching: Using a qualitative approach to connect homes and classrooms. *Theory into Practice, 31*(2), 132–141.

National Center for Cultural Competence. (2004). *Bridging the cultural divide in health care settings: The essential role of cultural broker programs.* Washington, DC: Georgetown University Center for Human Development.

Nevin, A., Smith, R., & McNeil, M. (2008). Shifting attitudes of related service providers: A disability studies and critical pedagogy approach. *International Journal of Whole Schooling, 4*(1), 1–12.

Newman, L. (2004). *Family involvement in the educational development of youth with disabilities: A special topic report from the National Longitudinal Transition Study-2 (NLTS-2).* Menlo Park, CA: SRI International.

Nixon, J. (2009). Exploring interaction between two distinct spheres of activism: Gender, disability and abuse. *Women's Studies International Forum, 32*(2), 142–149. doi. org/10.1016/j.wsif.2009.03.004

Olivos, E. M., Gallagher, R. J., & Aguilar, J. (2010). Fostering collaboration with culturally and linguistically diverse families of children with moderate to severe disabilities. *Journal of Educational and Psychological Consultation, 20*, 28–40. doi: 10.1080/10474410903535372

Ostiguy, B. J., Peters, M. L., & Shlasko, D. (2016). Ableism. In M. Adams & L. A. Bell (with D. J. Goodman & K. Y. Joshi) (Eds.), *Teaching for diversity and social justice* (3rd ed., pp. 299–228). New York, NY: Routledge.

Pacheco, M., & Gutiérrez, K. (2009). Cultural–historical approaches to literacy teaching and learning. In C. Compton-Lilly (Ed.), *Breaking the silence: Recognizing the social and cultural resources students bring to the classroom* (pp. 113–135). Delaware, MD: International Reading Association.

Pang, V. O., & Sablan, V. A. (1998). Teacher efficacy: How do teachers feel about their abilities to teach African American students? In M. E. Dilworth (Ed.), *Being responsive to cultural differences* (pp. 39–58). Thousand Oaks, CA: Corwin Press.

Resch, J. A., Mireles, G., Benz, M. R., Grenwelge, C., Peterson, R., & Zhang, D. (2010). Giving parents a voice: A qualitative study of the challenges experienced by parents of children with disabilities. *Rehabilitation Psychology, 55,* 139–150. doi:10.1037/a0019473

Rodriguez, D., Manner, J., & Darcy, S. (2010). Evolution of teacher perceptions regarding effective instruction for English language learners. *Journal of Hispanic Higher Education, 9*, 130–144.

Rossetti, Z., Burke, M. M., & Sauer, J. S. (2016, December). *Examining culturally and linguistically diverse families' engagement in the special education process.* Paper presented at the TASH Annual Conference: St. Louis, MO.

Rossetti, Z., Sauer, J. S., Bui, O., & Ou, S. (2017). Developing collaborative partnerships with culturally and linguistically diverse families during the IEP process. *Teaching Exceptional Children, 48*(5), 328–338.

Ryndak, D. L., Alper, S., Hughes, C., & McDonnell, J. (2012). Documenting impact of educational contexts on long-term outcomes for students with significant disabilities. *Education and Training in Autism and Developmental Disabilities, 47*(2), 127–138.

Sauer, J. S. (2012). "Look at me": Portraiture and agency. *Disability Studies Quarterly, 32*(4). Retrieved from dsq-sds.org/issue/view/98

Sauer, J. S., & Ferguson, P. (2013). Writing the global family, international perspectives on disability studies and family narratives. *Review of Disability Studies, 9*(2&3), 5–9.

Sauer, J. S., & Kasa, C. (2012). Preservice teachers listen to families of students with disabilities and learn a disability studies stance. *Issues in Teacher Education, 21*(2), 165–183.

Shapiro, J. P. (1993). *No pity: People with disabilities forging a new civil rights movement.* New York, NY: Times Books.

Skiba, R., Artiles, A. J., Kozleski, E. B., Losen, D., & Harry, B. (2016). Risks and consequences of oversimplifying educational inequities: A response to Morgan et al. (2015). *Educational Researcher, 45,* 221–225.

Solomon, M., Pistrang, N., & Barker, C. (2001). The benefits of mutual support groups for parents of children with disabilities. *American Journal of Community Psychology, 29,* 113–132. doi:10.1023/A:1005253514140

Steeley, S. L., & Lukacs, K. (2015). Cultural and linguistic diversity and special education: A case study of one mother's experiences. *International Journal of Special Education, 30,* 20–31.

Sullivan, A. L., & Bal, A. (2013). Disproportionality in special education: Effects of individual and school variables on risk. *Exceptional Children, 79,* 475–494.

Terrill, M., & Mark, D. (2000). Preservice teachers' expectations for schools with children of color and second language learners. *Journal of Teacher Education, 51,* 149–155.

Tiezzi, L. J., & Cross, B. E. (1997). Utilizing research on prospective teachers' beliefs to inform urban field experiences. *The Urban Review, 29,* 113–125.

Trainor, A. A. (2010). Educators' expectations of parent participation: The role of cultural and social capital. *Multiple Voices for Ethnically Diverse Exceptional Learners, 12,* 33–50. doi:10.5555/muvo.12.2.01x3497585xtw067

Trent, S. C., Kea, C. D., & Oh, K. (2008). Preparing preservice educators for cultural diversity: How far have we come? *Exceptional Children, 74,* 328–350.

Turnbull, A., Turnbull, R., Erwin, E. J., Soodak, L. C., & Shogren, K. A. (2011). *Families, professionals, and exceptionality: Positive outcomes through partnership and trust.* Boston, MA: Pearson.

U.S. Department of Education, National Center for Education Statistics. (2012). *The condition of education 2011* (NCES 2011-045). Washington, DC: Author.

U.S. Department of Education, National Institute on Disability and Rehabilitation Research (2006, February 15). *Notice of Final Long-Range Plan for Fiscal Years 2005–2009.* Washington, DC: Author. Retrieved from federalregister.gov/documents/2006/02/15/06-1255/national-institute-on-disability-and-rehabilitation-research-notice-of-final-long-range-plan-for

Wagner, M., Newman, L., Cameto, R., Javitz, H., & Valdes, K. (2012). A national picture of parent and youth participation in IEP and transition planning meetings. *Journal of Disability Policy Studies, 23,* 140–155. doi:10.1177/1044207311425384

Wolfe, K., & Duran, L. K. (2013). Culturally and linguistically diverse parents' perceptions of the IEP process: A review of current research. *Multiple Voices for Ethnically Diverse Exceptional Learners, 13(2),* 4–18.

Yosso, T. J. (2005). Whose culture has capital? A critical race theory discussion of community cultural wealth. *Race, Ethnicity, and Education, 8(1),* 69–91.

CHAPTER 2

"We Call Ourselves Chinese"
The Ou Family Portrait

Susan Ou and Janet Sauer

Susan[1] Ou laughs upon entering my (Janet's) university class of preservice special education teachers as she explains how trying to find a parking spot on the busy street near our urban campus delayed her arrival. Once again, she was volunteering her time to describe both her personal experiences as a Chinese immigrant mother of two boys involved in the American education system and her professional experiences as a cultural outreach broker for our state Parent Training and Information Center (PTI). More than a dozen times Susan has settled herself among university students to tell her story. She emphasizes that she does not represent the Chinese culture as one monolithic group identity, but rather that her story is "just a small piece."

SUSAN: "I'M A RISK TAKER."

"I lived in a big city in the southern part of China," Susan explains, and she met her Chinese American husband online through a relative. After 2 years of getting to know each other through email, Susan left college and her dream to become a lawyer to join her new husband and settle with his family in an urban center on the east coast of the United States. On that first international flight, her new husband remarked how willing she was to try everything offered, including the funny-shaped crackers (pretzels). Susan describes her American-born husband as more conservative and similar to the stereotypical Chinese "who goes along with the crowd," or who follows a Chinese custom of adapting to circumstances. By contrast, she calls herself a "risk taker," someone who respects her cultural norms but who recognizes her individuality and willingness to question the education system. She describes herself as someone who "understands the importance of supporting students' needs and parents' language access rights" (Asian Americans and Pacific Islanders, 2016). For 5 years, Susan has served as the Chinese Cultural

Outreach broker for the local PTI, organizing a parent support group and work-shops in Chinese for families of children with disabilities.

DEVELOPING CULTURAL UNDERSTANDING

Every time Susan talks about collaborating with families, she begins by empha-sizing the importance of "doing your research" about the family and their culture. Standing about five feet tall and donning glasses, Susan outlines three goals in her presentation to the class of university students: (1) understand Chinese fam-ily perspective, (2) recognize barriers and challenges families face, and (3) build collaboration between family and school. Susan describes common perspectives among the families with whom she has worked that she thinks are most important for teachers, particularly those without knowledge or personal experiences work-ing with Chinese families: "We think our children are the best, and they deserve the best education. We respect teachers and school, [and] we believe they will help us make our children achieve."

Months later in her office, Susan provides cultural context to these senti-ments: "About 3,000 years ago, our first teacher wrote a book that teaches us to respect hierarchy." The weight of that sentence hangs in the air as I consider the youth of Anglo-American culture and wonder what it might be like to have come from a place with such a long history. I admit to her having only a superficial understanding of China, and in my attempt to start to remedy the situation and to prepare for our meeting, I checked out a book from the local library titled *The Chinese* (Becker, 2000). Upon looking at the cover (a bright red background image of a crowd of men's faces behind another photograph of the Great Wall), Susan ex-claimed, "Wow, I can tell right away that's about the Cultural Revolution!" I won-dered, "What do my students and the teachers of immigrant children of Chinese families understand about this time in history? What impact, if any, might the Cultural Revolution have on efforts to develop collaborative relationships between teachers of children identified as disabled by the American education system and their families who may have personal experience?" I grew up in the 1960s and 1970s when Mao Zedong, Chairman of the Communist Party, set out to have its youth "purge the 'impure' elements of Chinese society. . . . The Cultural Revolution continued in various phases until Mao's death in 1976, and its tormented and vi-olent legacy would resonate in Chinese politics and society for decades to come" (www.history.com/topics/china/cultural-revolution).

"In Chinese culture," Susan surmises aloud, "and other Asian cultures that have such long histories, we are adaptable. That's how we've survived." She under-stands that American schools, particularly special education, expect parents to become advocates for their children. "Here is not China," she tells other Chinese immigrants whose children are entitled to services under the Individuals with Disabilities Education Act (IDEA). She continues to explain, "In Chinese culture the assumption is that the teacher knows [everything] and we know nothing [as parents], which is why we're so passive." Susan says that seeking a career in education in China is like becoming a doctor because their teacher education is so highly rigorous. Thus the American special education process in which teachers might begin a meeting by asking the family questions may result in confusion or even skepticism that the teacher is qualified because he or she should not need to ask the family questions.

CHINESE FAMILY DIVERSITY

As a cultural outreach broker for the Chinese community, Susan wants school professionals to understand the individuality of each child and his or her family. "We all call ourselves Chinese, but because of the dialect[2] and also because of the geographic culture, we are slightly different in how we project. How we take care of our children with special needs will be slightly different." Susan explains that some families come from different geographic and demographic backgrounds that could influence their understanding of American culture and the English language; some families are Christian and "may emphasize loving relationships, while other families may be Buddhist and emphasize discipline." Some families include a mother with a higher education level that could mean she is expected to do the research into finding and arranging the logistics (travel, health insurance) for the children while also working.

STUDENT REFLECTION: The perspective Susan is sharing is only one Chinese perspective, and truly only one person's perspective. We should never assume you know someone based on what you have heard/learned. Always be open-minded. —Undergraduate student

---

Susan describes how the extended family is often directly involved in raising children and in decisionmaking. "Many Chinese immigrant families are working multiple jobs as they struggle to have a quality of life . . . they come [to America] for different purposes." She points out that for some families their quality of life would have been better back in China where the entire community would have provided support to one another. In her own close-knit family, although her parents live in China, they remain involved by frequent FaceTiming, and Susan is planning a summer family visit to China. During one of her visits to my class, the students and I co-constructed Susan's "circle of supports" (O'Brien & O'Brien, 2002; see Figure 2.1 on p. 30). It began with her boys' names in the middle, and then included her, their father (Will), her parents, Will's parents, teachers, peers, sports teams, and therapists. She added friends of her in-laws who live nearby, one cousin, and a babysitter who is "a Chinese grandma who speaks Mandarin." She noted that these supports change over time.

CHINESE IMMIGRATION

Learning about Chinese history and waves of immigration from China into the United States is valuable to understanding many of the families that school personnel work with, particularly when the extended family is involved. While most American teachers are familiar with the many Chinese immigrants who built the transcontinental railroad, few may know that "competition with American workers and a growing nativism brought pressure for restrictive action which began with the [Chinese Exclusion] Act of May 6, 1882," suspending Chinese immigration for the next decade (www.archives.gov/research/chinese-americans/guide). Additional exclusionary legislation followed, such as the Geary Act of 1892, which required registration papers for Chinese immigrants with penalties of prison or deportation. Chinese immigrants themselves often enforced such policies. Although FDR lifted some restrictions during WWII, it was not until the Immigration Act of 1965 that Chinese immigrants were given more equitable opportunities for naturalization.

According to U.S. Census data, New York City, San Francisco, and Los Angeles have some of the largest Chinese American populations, but there are large numbers of Chinese Americans living in other cities in California, Texas, New Jersey, Massachusetts, Illinois, Washington, and Pennsylvania.[3] Most cities have seen a steady increase in waves of immigrants for a variety of reasons. For instance, in Boston the 1880 census counted over 110,000 immigrants, most of whom were Irish and emigrated because of a famine in their home country. More recent data indicate that Asian and Latino populations increased more than 65% from 1990 to 2000, and more than 33% of the city's population was reported as speaking a language in addition to English: "Boston speaks 140 languages" (Jimenez, 2019, p. 2).

SCHOOL AND FAMILY ENGAGEMENT: "DO SOME RESEARCH."

Federal law requires states to provide free and appropriate education to all children regardless of their immigration status (U.S. Courts, 2019). During President Trump's tenure, news reports suggest confusion about this policy and its impact on educating immigrant children (e.g., NYC Mayor's Office of Immigrant Affairs, "Know your rights: Federal immigration enforcement," 2019). In response, some states are developing resources for educational professionals and culturally and linguistically diverse families. Boston Public Schools, for example, with which Susan works, created a website called BPS: We Dream Together (sites.google.com/bostonpublicschools .org/bpswedreamtogether), providing immigration resources in 15 languages. One school committee chair is quoted as saying, "We must ensure that our schools remain safe and secure places for our immigrant students and their families." The site also states, "Boston Public Schools is proud to be one of the most diverse school districts in the nation with nearly half of all students speaking a language other than English at home, representing 139 different native countries."

According to a recent demography report from the Boston Mayor's office, "Nearly one-quarter of all Massachusetts children are either immigrants or the children of immigrants" (Jimenez, 2019, p. 3). Language diversity is particularly relevant to the assessment and diagnosis process of children labeled as at risk or suspected of having a disability. Of the procedural safeguards outlined in IDEA, language diversity plays a key role in the requirement for family engagement. Current data suggest that many of these children are of Chinese families and make up "the largest foreign-born group in the region" (globalboston.bc.edu/index.php/home/ethnic-groups/).

Although Susan says that in Chinese culture, "academic[s] is everything," many of the Chinese families she works with are "tough to engage" because they expect teachers to take care of everything involving academics. In her experience, Chinese families tend not to ask questions of teachers because "teachers are the experts and presumed to know everything." Additionally, Susan points out that many parents are both working and therefore they cannot take off work to go to the school for a meeting. However, she encourages teachers to find a way to have a face-to-face meeting because it is better than other methods of communicating. In her tips, she invites teachers to "maintain a harmonious environment, respect hierarchy, and pay compliments" in order to build meaningful relationships.

Each time Susan visits one of my classes I learn something more from and about her. While she repeats the importance of respecting *the teacher*, she acknowledges there are times when parents may have questions or disagree with the school's recommendations. This tension is the most unsettling for the Chinese families with whom she works. She focused a discussion on a common Chinese cultural norm of avoiding refusals. This tendency can lead to parents and guardians signing what school personnel might think of as affirming permission for services or placement, but without understanding or because they would not want to engage in conflict. Susan describes this issue further:

> Please understand, as parents, we always think our child is the best, and
> therefore deserves the best educational service. That is why you will see
> that parent will be strong fighting for that support. Particular[ly, parents]
> in the north will fight for high[er] education. Even if we have a child with
> special needs, we will push our child to help them. If we have children with
> intellectual disabilities or autism, we have really high expectations. We really
> respect the teacher. Most of the time you'll see when you have a meeting
> with Chinese families, even if they disagree with what you say, they will just
> nod their heads. And don't want to say anything negative. They are more
> passive. They just keep saying yes, even though in their minds they disagree.
> And that creates a challenge because in America we always advocate for
> the idea that if you empower yourself, if you disagree you can speak up, but
> in our culture, we are not allowed to say that because the teacher, in our
> opinion, will always help the child.

Regarding homework, Susan provides an explanation from her own childhood that influences her current expectations for her children. She believes homework is the child's responsibility:

> We will push ourselves and our children. I know here if a student cannot finish, a parent can talk to the teacher and it can be extended, but for us, if you have one page of homework today, you will finish it. That's your responsibility, regardless. You have to finish before you can do some other fun thing like watch a movie or TV or play. You have to finish your homework.

She tells me to look in Chinatown and I will see advertisements everywhere for tutors who can help children complete homework. Since so many parents are working multiple jobs and cannot transport their children for support services, Susan explains, "they will sometimes ask for certain services that are uncommon for other parents," like transportation to tutoring.

When trying to find information to support their children with what Susan refers to as "special needs," some parents do not know where to look, and other times it is simply a language barrier. "As you know, if you go to any resource it is mostly English, maybe some Spanish. For Chinese, now it's getting a bit better, but we still need a lot more done to translate the materials." Like others working with families who are learning English, Susan recommends that proofreading is necessary, especially by someone with expertise in the field of special education, because a direct word-for-word translation is not helpful for parents to understand the meaning behind the words:

> We have so many misperceptions for Chinese cultures and I just want you to know because the family perspective is really different from the law, based on the dialect, or based on the education, or even how the culture plays a role. So even though we are all called Chinese, sometimes you will see that a family from China's mainland is slightly different than the parent from Taiwan or the parent who is [from] Hong Kong.

Susan's work as a cultural outreach broker with other Chinese families of children with disabilities led her to notice that some are willing to seek help while others are not. "Parents in our culture are very self-judgmental. If a teacher asks about things happening at home, then the parent will think, 'Oh no! I must be doing something wrong! I'm not doing my job!'"

STUDENT REFLECTION: I love this quote! I think this idea is so important, whether or not an educator is communicating with a parent from another culture. A stigma that surrounds special education is that it is either the parents' fault or the child's fault. I feel like anytime an educator is communicating with the family it needs to be stressed that a disability is not a reflection of parenting ability or family dynamics. —Undergraduate student

---

Susan clarifies how different Chinese immigrant families have settled in different parts of the country, and they might bring with them cultural variations from their communities within China. Even within the same American city, Chinese immigrant communities may differ in their dominant language dialect. Though there are the two main dialects (oral languages)—Mandarin and Cantonese—there are many others depending on where the families emigrated from. She said that within the nearest Chinatown you can also hear Taishanese and Fujanese: "Pretty much everywhere has their own dialect. They sound similar to Mandarin or Cantonese, but it can take a while to distinguish, even as a Chinese speaker." This is important to consider when school personnel are looking for someone to interpret language in a meeting. It can also be something families and professionals will discern among themselves, possibly establishing social hierarchies that undoubtedly influences their communication.

When school personnel are looking for someone to translate written words, there are special considerations as well. Susan explains that spoken dialects are important, but written Chinese also has multiple versions: *simplified* and *traditional* Chinese. "I am the lucky one, because I know both, but most parents only recognize one." It depends on the wave of immigrants the family came with. Even when a district might hire someone to translate the written words, Susan emphasizes the importance of having someone with education knowledge proofread it or it may not make sense to the parents. "Word-for-word translation, to parents, really has no meaning." For example, there is no concept in Chinese for applied behavior analysis. She further points out that just as there are differences in the spoken and written Chinese languages, there are variations of families' approaches to care for their children: "Because of the dialect and geographic culture [back in China] we are slightly different in how we take care of the child with special needs."

"We are so complicated that before you talk with a parent, I would like you to do some research." Find out which dialect and which form of written language the family knows. Susan emphasizes creativity: a general education teacher might need to give 100% effort, but "if you are a special education teacher, I think you need to put 150% of your effort" for the student to make progress. "I think one of the challenges is that each child is unique. You can't use one curriculum or method to teach, even if they have the same diagnosis. You have to go beyond your expectations. I think we all do." She goes on to say that we also need to think about the future so the student can live well in his community; "I think that is critical."

To review, Susan shared several insights into Chinese immigrant family cultural communication nuances. While emphasizing the uniqueness of every family, she advises teachers to try face-to-face conversations and reach out to local cultural brokers to find out which dialects and languages the families use for oral and written communication. When interacting with families, Susan wants school and service providers to understand the powerful cultural norms of relinquishing educational decisions to the teacher. Even if families nod their heads in response to a request, they may disagree but want to avoid conflict. Because of these sociocultural norms, it is a rare occasion when a family asks a question or disagrees, so when they do, "please understand" how hard that is for them. Susan suggests professionals can learn about the people in their students' circles of support (see Figure 2.1), to better understand the demands on the family's time (e.g., if they are working multiple jobs to help pay for tutors). The value of doing research for developing positive relationships with Chinese families cannot be overstated, especially when professionals suspect a child has a disability.

THE ASSESSMENT AND DIAGNOSIS PROCESS:
"A KID IS A WHOLE PERSON."

During her presentations, Susan highlights the complexity involved when young children raised in bilingual homes in the United States are expected to become proficient English speakers, readers, and writers. She speaks from firsthand experience with these obstacles as she describes the complexity of her sons' diagnoses. She shared photographs of her two young boys—Bruce and Ian—and the school assessments and reports she has received over the years about each of them. At different ages, both of her children were referred for special education evaluations (Bruce at 2.9 and Ian at 3.1 years old) that resulted in early intervention and special education services. In one presentation as a guest speaker, Susan emphasized the importance of understanding the whole child during the assessment and diagnosis process, taking into account a variety of perspectives and resources. She said, "We don't think that just one resource is enough. A kid is a whole person."

Figure 2.1. Susan's Circle of Support

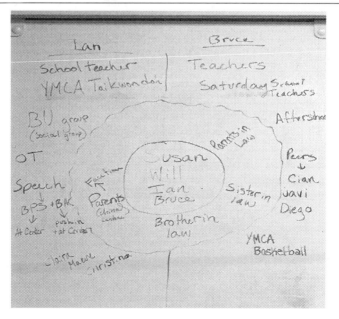

Photo 2.1. Ian, 4 Years Old, Reading a Book with One of the College Students

During one more recent university visit in which Susan brought both of her boys with her, my undergraduate students noticed how readily the boys warmed up to them. The boys talked (in English) so much with the college students that their voices often obscured my interview with Susan, making it difficult to later transcribe the recording. During their class visit, some of my students took observation notes and photographs while others read books and played games with Susan's boys (see Photo 2.1). These positive social interactions contrasted with the clinical, deficit-oriented assessment process and paperwork.

STUDENT REFLECTION: It would be cool to do an observation within their home. I wonder, "How is their culture/Cantonese culture implemented within the home (language, food, customs, decorations)? What are the children's (Bruce and Ian) personal connection to their language/culture?" —Undergraduate student

---

Bruce

When we first began our project, Susan described her older son, Bruce, then a toddler, as "a typical, happy boy" who likes to play with toy cars and balls." She added, "He is a big fan of Thomas and Friends, Elmo, and Curious George." When he described himself to my class as a 2nd-grader, he talked about helping his teammate score while playing soccer and then added, "I'm a fan of the Celtics!" A socially adept child, Bruce was quick to recruit one of the college students to help him practice his spelling for the next day's test, and then he joined his brother in playing several games with the group of college students (see Photo 2.2).

During a different university class visit Susan pointed to a photo of Bruce donning a T-shirt (see Photo 2.3) and announced, "That's my older son when

Photo 2.2. Bruce Playing the Money Game with a College Student

Photo 2.3. Bruce as a Toddler at Home

he was 3 years old going to pre-K; now he's in 1st grade. Bruce is a kid with a language delay." In reference to his assessment and evaluation process as a toddler, Susan explained that when Bruce was 1½ years old, a nurse asked several questions, one of which was "How many words does he speak [in any language]?" When Susan and her husband responded, "Not that much," the nurse asked additional questions about Bruce's developmental milestones. With the nurse's encouragement, they sought out an evaluation. Yet Susan and her family "struggled" with the process, "even though I was working in my [professional] position." She explained, "Your parent hat always overrides your professional hat." She struggled not only with the special education system, trying to negotiate the process and communicate with the professionals, but also with her extended family's dismissive response: "I was hearing my mother-in-law's opinion [reflected] in our culture [where] it is believed that boys tend to be slower to develop their language skills." Eventually, Bruce was evaluated and determined to be entitled to speech services from an early interventionist, but since "he made so much progress, he was ineligible to continue" upon turning 3 years old. His parents thought Bruce should continue with services, so they advocated for another evaluation.

Bruce's evaluation involved a bilingual speech language pathologist who used the PLS-5 (Preschool Language Scale, 5th edition) and observations of oral motor mechanisms and articulators (teeth, lips, tongue). Her report indicated age-appropriate auditory comprehension skills, representational play, and accurate expressive language, while noting no history of hearing issues. Bruce's parents were told that "because he is a bilingual student," it was "normal" for him to go through a "silent period." While her judgment reflects related research in multi/bilingual assessment for children referred for special education, this distinction between disability and language is complicated, and opinions vary on its efficacy in practice (see Klingner & Eppolito, 2014; Serpa, 2019).

Over the years, Susan has developed a strong opinion about the use of the family's home language:

> The child has been listening to that language since before they were born, when they were in their mom's belly. That language is their foundation and [to] do something else, the parents won't have the skills to help build up their children. Think of it like a building. You take off the foundation and add something new at the top, do you think it will be very stable? From my own experience from my younger and my older son, it's helpful for them to learn a second language, a third or fourth language. Because they already have the skills and the foundation, and they have the confidence as well, now they can learn. But if you take off their foundation, their home language, their mother tongue, that means that they are lacking something to carry across and help them learn another language.

She explains that if a professional discourages the use of the home language, it could be even more problematic for the child, particularly if the child needs to develop communication and social skills. Imagine the family conversation in Chinese, but the child with disabilities is not allowed to speak it; they could be further pushed away from building relationships, even those within the family. "Just ask the family," Susan tells my class, because "all children have the ability to learn and can become bilingual." In fact, both of her children are multilingual, and many children with disabilities grow up and become bi- or multilingual.

Ian

When describing her younger son (at age 5), Susan explained that Ian is quick to figure things out. With a laugh, she provides the example of when they hide his favorite snack (potato chips)—he can always find them. "Even after many days, he still remembers. If we try to distract him, he will figure it out immediately." He is interested in toy cars (especially Hot Wheels) and playing with his friends. He avoids physical sports and does not like others getting into his personal space. Susan said that when he was about 3 years old, he would drop to the floor upset if someone took his toys, but at 5 years old he can use his words. During his visit to my class, Ian dictated the list of school rules to one of the college students, and wrote out some of them himself.

Like his older brother, Bruce, Ian grew up in a multilingual family. His grand-parents speak Cantonese, while his parents speak "a mixture" of Cantonese and English. Ian attended an English-speaking preschool. Since his communication skills were "further along" than Bruce's, the family did not seek early intervention. However, the family and his teacher requested an evaluation as he entered preschool because of his preference for interactions with adults and parallel play with peers. It was determined that he had a "developmental delay," and an IEP was created.

In an initial speech and language evaluation when Ian was nearly 4 years old, Ian's father, Will, reported that while he speaks English to his son, Susan speaks Chinese to him. The report indicates that Ian will "frequently switch between lan-guages when speaking, utilizing both English and Chinese words within the same utterance no matter what language his communication partner is speaking." A bi-lingual speech–language pathologist (SLP) had already assessed Ian and determined that he was eligible for services for "self-regulation skills within the classroom." However, the report states: "Ian's parents do not agree with the proposed service recommendations made by [the district] and have therefore not enrolled Ian yet."

The report includes results from psychological tests (e.g., BAYLEY, BASC, ABAS); informal observations; and the CELF-Preschool 2 standardized test for expressive, receptive, pragmatic language, articulation, and oral motor skills, indi-cating some concern with fluency ("atypical prosody, including variable rate and intonation"). The report stated:

> It is important to note that Ian's speech occasionally became unintelligible
> as he produced longer utterances. However, Ian was noted to sometimes
> include Chinese words within his mostly English utterances, which may
> have impacted the clinician's difficulty understanding some long utterances.
> Therefore, Ian's speech sound intelligibility should be further explored
> in subsequent sessions. . . . Based on the results of today's evaluation, Ian
> presents with delays in receptive language, expressive language, and pragmatic
> language/play skills. He would benefit from speech–language intervention.

The report ruled out other issues; he did not have any major illnesses or ac-cidents, and although he had several ear infections during his first year, more re-cent tests of hearing acuity were considered "normal." Ian's cognitive skills were described as "average" with "low average social and emotional skill areas." His motoric milestones were also determined to follow typical development. A com-prehensive list of seven areas of concern was included in the report, highlighting deficit areas, with only brief mention of any strengths. One sentence was essential-ly buried: "Ian demonstrated use of a large vocabulary and age-appropriate length of utterances." They recommended a language-rich environment that could offer opportunities to engage with age-matched peers in a "structured setting," along with direct speech services 30 minutes per week.

When discussing Ian's IEP with one of my classes, Susan recalled getting regular calls from his kindergarten teacher expressing concerns about Ian's behavior and communication. Sometimes he would not take a nap along with the other children and was disrupting them, or he would not share the toys. Other times, the teacher did not think Ian understood English. The school counselor and teacher told her that their private school would not be able to offer Ian special services, so they would need to look at the public schools. Susan said that at home they also had some concerns about his use of gestures rather than words to communicate. However, they thought some of the reason behind his behavior may have been a natural part of the transition from day care to school. The bilingual family day care center staff spoke Cantonese, but some of his friends spoke Mandarin, while at home they were speaking Cantonese, Mandarin, and English. In Ian's school, they only spoke English to him.

Susan's family has been involved with the special education system for most of their children's lives. Even with some social and cultural capital in terms of Susan's work and connections with professionals in the field, she describes the process as "challenging." In addition to helping other families of children involved in special education, Susan is committed to building a collaborative relationship with her children's teachers and others in their circles of support. Since arriving in the United States, Susan has spent several years learning about the American approach to schooling, coordinating communication and services for her children, and advocating for equitable and meaningful supports for families in the Chinese community.

STUDENT REFLECTION: I can't even imagine how difficult this must be to understand coming from such a different education system. It would probably be easier for the families to get used to if they had other families in similar situations surrounding them. I can imagine the family support groups are an amazing support for families to become integrated in their communities. —Undergraduate student

---

CONCLUSION

Family-school communication and collaboration can be rewarding but also challenging. We set out to write strengths-based portraits of culturally and linguistically diverse families with a goal of improving these relationships for the sake of the children' learning and development. It is a shared goal for both families and school professionals to support the progress of these children, and yet even with so many years of research and professional development in the area, we continue to struggle. It became clear while reviewing the Ou children's files, the interview transcripts, and related research articles that the special education system as it is currently organized causes conflict between CLD families and schools. Families are assumed to have the cultural and linguistic knowledge, technical vocabulary, and comfort with directly challenging teachers (something antithetical to some families' cultural beliefs) that are expected in order to engage in the IEP process. School personnel, and particularly preservice professionals, are not educated beyond the surface level about specific cultural histories of majority immigrant populations; they are not required to learn a second language themselves, a skill that could help develop empathy, understanding, and cultural humility; and IEPs about CLD families are not written from a strengths-based orientation. Susan's three points described in this chapter state goals seeking greater understanding and collaboration among families of children who find themselves involved in the special education process and the professionals hired to support them.

REFLECTION QUESTIONS

- After reading Susan's story, would you agree with the following student's reflection? Why or why not?

    "I feel like Susan's personal story and interaction with the barrier between culture and services for her son were very meaningful and important. Up until this point Susan had given general information about the services available through the [PTI] for parents of children with special needs, as well as given us some common thought processes among Chinese parents. However, having her tell her story, and how she struggled with her family and getting support for her son, even though she worked in an outreach support service for children with special needs, was very eye opening and made the abstract barriers we were learning about much more concrete."

- What was familiar to you, and what new information did you learn from Susan's story?
- If you were to work with Susan's family, what else might you want to know that was missing from the portrait, or that you hoped to learn more about? Can you brainstorm possible reasons why some information might be absent? How could you seek out the information you would like to learn?
- When thinking about language development for children acquiring multiple languages like Bruce and Ian, it is important to consider the biases each person brings to the special education process. Take this opportunity to assess your own sense of cultural awareness, competence, and humility (see Chapter 8's section on Personal Action Plan for Change). Consider also the training, coursework, and philosophical stance of each professional; a speech language pathologist, for instance, may not have depth in bilingual language acquisition studies.

NOTES

1. When she worked at an international company in China before coming to the United States (2004–2007), Susan was told to choose an English name, so she chose *Susan*. When asked repeatedly if she would like us to use her given name, June Yu, in the book, she insisted, "Just use Susan." For further reading about the issues of using a given name or assimilation, see Huang (2017) and Skerry (2000).

2. Over 100 languages are spoken in China, with a variety of dialects among more than 50 ethnic groups. For more information, see chinahighlights.com/travelguide/article-chinese-language-facts.htm

3. "The Census Bureau collects race data according to U.S. Office of Management and Budget guidelines, and these data are based on self-identification. People may choose to report more than one race group. People of any race may be of any ethnic origin." Retrieved from www.census.gov/topics/population/race.html

REFERENCES

Asian Americans and Pacific Islanders. (2016, October 21). *Biography of Susan Ou for The Rights to Education Panel for AAPI Communities.* Retrieved from https://aapicivilrights forum2016.sched.com/speaker/susan_ou.1vpppeoa

Becker, J. (2000). *The Chinese: An insider's look at the issues which affect and shape China today.* New York, NY: Free Press.

Huang, Z. (2017, February 14). *After being James, Peter, and William, I decided to stick with my Chinese name.* Retrieved from qz.com/908929/after-being-james-peter-and-william-i-decided-to-stick-with-my-chinese-name/

Jimenez, C. R. (2019). *New Bostonians demographic report.* City of Boston Mayor's Office. Retrieved from cityofboston.gov/newbostonians/pdfs/dem_report.pdf

Klingner, J., & Eppolito, A. M. (2014). *English language learners: Differentiating between language acquisition and learning disabilities.* Arlington, VA: Council for Exceptional Children.

NYC Mayor's Office of Immigrant Affairs. (2019, July 12). Know your rights: Federal immigration enforcement. Retrieved from www1.nyc.gov/site/immigrants/help/legal-services/deportation-defense.page

O'Brien, J., & O'Brien, C. L. (Eds.). (2002). *Implementing person-centered planning: Voices of experience* (Vol. II). Toronto, Canada: Inclusion Press.

Serpa, M. (2019). *An imperative for change: Bridging special and language learning education to ensure a free and appropriate education in the least restrictive environment for ELLs with disabilities in Massachusetts.* Boston, MA: University of Massachusetts, Gastón Institute Publications.

Skerry, P. (2000, March 1). *Do we really want immigrants to assimilate?* The Brookings Institution. Retrieved from brookings.edu/articles/do-we-really-want-immigrants-to-assimilate.

U.S. Courts. (2019). Access to education—Rule of Law. Retrieved from www.uscourts.gov/educational-resources/educational-activities/access-education-rule-law

CHAPTER 3

"A Girl Who Has Beauty Inside and Out"

A Portrait of a Vietnamese Mother and Daughter

Oanh Thi Thu Bui, with Zach Rossetti

> She loves watching videos on YouTube.
> She loves to read, although she won't read anything twice.
> She loves music.
> She loves to dance.
> She speaks two languages—Vietnamese and English.
> She's creative in getting her point across.
> She gets frustrated when she can't get that point across.
> She always remembers her "pleases and thank-yous."
> She's a very active little girl.
> Her name is Tiny.
>
> —written by a graduate student in special education
> after Oanh presented in the second author's (Zach's) class

Thinking back to when I, Oanh, first came to the United States and later, when my daughter Tiny joined me, gives me chills. I do not know how I did it and what I did that I could have lasted until today. Through my own experiences and my work with many underserved families, I decided to share my personal journey of accessing services for my daughter. I wrote this for educators working with children and youth with disabilities, and other parents and caregivers whose first language is not English, whose children happen to have different needs, and who might not be familiar with advocacy and how the system works. It has been a journey full of roadblocks, but I feel blessed to be able to share my personal stories. I hope my experiences can provide a better picture of what the majority of immigrant families are dealing with in the special education system and what we can all do differently to reach our common goals of improving student outcomes and supporting parent engagement as equal team members.

IMMIGRATING TO THE UNITED STATES

As parents, we all have high expectations for our children even before they are born. I named my daughter Nguyen Tam Song Thu, which has a deep meaning in Vietnamese: "a girl who has beauty inside and out, intelligence, and a good heart." Just like any other parent, I want to see a bright future for my child as a successful citizen of society, no matter where she lives. However, things are not always as we planned.

I called her Tiny because she was tiny when she was born. Tiny weighed just 4 pounds, and because she was often sick, she spent much of her time at home with a nanny. At 3½ years old, she could not walk or talk. During her first five years in Vietnam, no public or private schools would accept her because of her differences. I searched for help despite limited services and a cultural attitude that those with difficulties will outgrow them. Tiny's grandparents and many neighbors said, "Just know not to be worried. She's fine. Many kids can't talk until they're 7 or 9." In addition, we did not have any speech pathologists in Vietnam back then, so there was no professional input to consider. Seeking doctors who knew more about Tiny's medical, physical, and psychological complexities was like finding a needle in the haystack.

Fortunately, when Tiny was 3 years old, I was awarded a Ford Foundation scholarship to attend graduate school in the United States. That was a big opportunity for me. It took me a full year to make the decision to leave for the Boston area. It was challenging to make that decision because traditionally in Vietnam as a married woman, you are expected to stay home and take care of your child and family. After much reflection, I decided to leave Tiny with my husband and extended family in Vietnam and head to the United States. I was worried about her future. I had taken her to many hospitals in Vietnam, and we had not found any answers, and I could not support her on my own. I needed answers to her problems to help her in the long run.

I hoped to be able to kill two birds with one stone: complete my master's degree and have Tiny seen by American medical providers at the end of my graduate degree. I strongly believed the advanced medical system in the United States could help me understand what was going on with her and provide me with an intervention plan, and then we would return to Vietnam. I was so grateful for this golden opportunity.

Eventually, Tiny joined me in the United States at 5½ years old. Tiny still could not speak, did not walk much, understood no English, was very active (e.g., she could hardly sit still, she moved around constantly, she would pull things on the floor), and was hardly able to eat solid foods. I carried her on my shoulders to and from public transportation and around the university campus (see Photo 3.1). I carried a thermos of pureed soup to be sure she was not starving, as she could not tell me if she was hungry nor understand how to eat American foods. Since I did not have family or the financial resources to help with child care, I recruited some wonderful classmates to care for Tiny while I completed assignments and prepared for classes (see Photo 3.2).

Photo 3.1 Tiny
Being Carried
from Home
to the Bus
Station

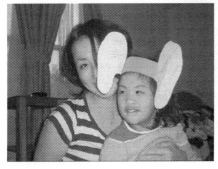

Photo 3.2. Auntie Ai Morita,
My Classmate, Taking Care
of Tiny While I Was at School

STUDENT REFLECTION: Oanh wanted to do everything possible for Tiny. Leaving her at home and with family in Vietnam was not easy. I noticed the tears in her eyes as she talked about how she hasn't seen her family in person since moving to the United States in 2008. —Graduate student

CULTURAL CONTEXT: VIETNAM

Most readers likely know of the Vietnam War. In 1975, at the end of the war, the United States sponsored about 125,000 Vietnamese refugees to relocate in the United States. Since then the Vietnamese immigrant population has continued to grow. In 2017 there were 1.3 million Vietnamese living in the United States; this is 3% of all immigrants and represents the sixth-largest immigrant group in the country (Alperin & Batalova, 2018).

Many readers may not be aware that the Chinese colonized Vietnam for 1,000 years, and the French colonized Vietnam for 100 years. Chinese influence in the form of Confucian, Taoist, and Laotist traditions, including respect for adults and the value of education, last today. It is said that first is scholar, second farmer, third is business; thus education is vital in Vietnamese communities. The Education Law of the Socialist Republic of Vietnam states explicit goals to teach all students: To respect, love, and show good behaviors toward grandparents, parents, teachers, and elders; to love brothers, sisters, and friends; and to be sincere, confident, eager to learn, and appreciate nature's beauty (Vietnamese Ministry of Education, 2006). Parents are proud of their children's success and will do all they can to ensure that their children go to good schools. My parents fostered this in our family. They know that only with education can I get out of a tough life working in the garden. I remember vividly my dad saying, "You need to speak English well so you can reach a new horizon and change your life."

The concept of losing face also reflects the importance of the Vietnamese collective culture (Truong, Hallinger, & Sanga, 2017). People modify their behaviors and attitudes to fit with the conception of their primary group associations. Misconduct or failure of an individual to meet the communal expectation or standard is a reflection on one's parents, siblings, and ancestors. For example, Borton (2000) stresses that "loss of face is painful in any society, but unbearable in Vietnam" (p. 24). This prevents many Vietnamese parents from taking kids with disabilities out in public due to social stigma. The social stigma and loss of face related to disability result in fear that the whole community will look down on their family or blame their ancestors, which can be very insulting for Vietnamese parents. Thus many families feel compelled to hide their children's disabilities. Conversely, success, fame, or achievement by an individual brings honor and pride to the family and one's communal association (Bich, 1999). Thus Vietnamese society reflects collectivism in its social culture.

MULTIPLE DIAGNOSES, MULTIPLE MEANINGS ACROSS CULTURES

In addition to my graduate workload and a part-time job, I spent as much time as possible learning about the American medical, educational, and social support systems and how my daughter could access what she needs for her physical, mental, and educational growth to allow her to lead an independent life. Compared to interacting with only one doctor in Vietnam, I learned to collaborate with multiple hospitals and school teams, as well as numerous therapists and other specialists (see Figure 3.1). The Care Map illustrates several areas of care—school, health, recreation/community, legal/financial—each of which involved a number of different providers and professionals. After identifying a high number of professionals, it often took months to schedule appointments with them. Further, I found that these professionals often did not share information with one another. I had to synthesize all of the reports and recommendations, which were in English, my second language. Navigating the U.S. medical system was extremely difficult.

Generally, communicating with these professionals was another challenge. Phone operators, particularly automated ones, could not understand my accent. I spent hours trying to contact people who could understand me, just to get assessments Tiny needed to access the supports and services that would help her. I also asked my classmates and friends who spoke English with less of an accent to make calls with or for me. Of course, once assessments began, there was so

Figure 3.1. Care Map Showing the Number of Professionals That Oanh Needs to Interact with in Caring for Her Daughter, Tiny

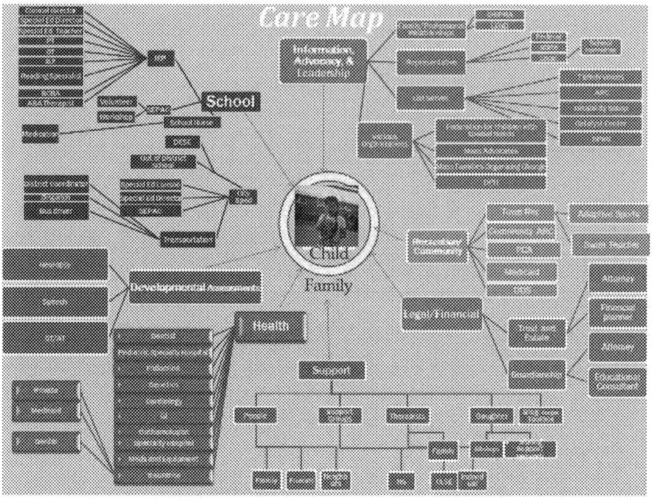

Adapted from Care Map by Cristin Lind (2012).

much paperwork (e.g., assessment results, medical reports, insurance forms), all in English. This was very different from Vietnam, where Tiny did not have any medical records. Making sense of it all and organizing documents for future reference became quite a job in itself!

I am thankful for the opportunity to access the more advanced medical, educational, and physical care in the United States. First, Tiny was diagnosed with autism spectrum disorder when she was 6 years old. I knew nothing about autism at the time and strove to learn everything I could about it. I spent hours searching online, attending any presentations I could, and building my own library of resources. I tried to explain autism to my family in Vietnam, but they did not understand the nature of a lifelong developmental disability, especially one that was "invisible," one that did not come with a physical impairment. They focused only on when Tiny would be cured by the American doctors, asking, "Can she talk now?" For me, they seemed to be asking, "When will we see the results of your years away from home?" and "When are you returning home?"

Through graduate school connections and countless calls to hospitals, I scheduled Tiny for an MRI. This led to a diagnosis of two rare chromosomal duplication disorders: Kabuki syndrome, which causes low muscle tone, among other symptoms, and 15q13.3 microduplication, which results in developmental delays. These conditions were thought to cause Tiny's medical, physical, and psychological complexities. I studied these conditions so I could best help her. However, I realized it is most important to see the child first, not the disability. Look at their strengths, look at their potential, and try to build them up.

STUDENT REFLECTION: Although Tiny may have similar characteristics as others with autism and chromosomal abnormalities, her mother's wish is for people to look at Tiny as an individual first. It is very common for people with disabilities to get locked into a diagnosis, and some teachers forget to get to know the individual. —Graduate student

NAVIGATING THE SPECIAL EDUCATION SYSTEM

The fact that my daughter could go to school and participate in many activities meant a lot to me. This was her very first chance to access educational opportunities, in addition to receiving proper medical care.

I was overwhelmed at the very first Individualized Education Program (IEP) meeting for my daughter, being there all by myself among the wonderful team of professionals with whom I had no relationship yet. I believed back then that they would do what was best for Tiny. Culturally, we believe that teachers will do what they can to support children. As a parent, my role is to feed her, to provide a safe, comfortable space for her to live, and to maintain her well-being. Literacy and education are left for the teacher and the school. I knew English enough to communicate and finish my graduate courses, but came to realize I was not proficient enough in the technical language of special education. This seemed like a foreign language for me back then, with so many terms that I had never heard of and with so much jargon. I was asked to sign the 20-page IEP right after the IEP meeting, without even fully understanding what it said, but knew my signature would start the services for her. Yet all that stayed with me after that meeting was the question: Should I continue to speak to my daughter in Vietnamese?

The speech-language pathologist (SLP) was clear as she told me, "You should stop speaking Vietnamese to your daughter. She will be around all English-speaking peers and teachers. It will just confuse her since she is a nonverbal child." The SLP went on to imply that I was taking things for granted and using tax dollars for my child's benefit. My daughter had been at school in the United States for about 2 months at that point. As a single mom who was unfamiliar with the educational, medical, and social support systems in the United States, I was feeling frustrated while navigating the system of care and support for my child. Hearing that opinion from a professional gave me chills. Asking a parent to stop speaking to her child in her mother tongue is like asking a child who is blind not to use Braille or a child who is deaf not to use sign language. This confused me and led me to different trainings on parental rights, which helped me understand my role as a parent within the provision of special education and related services mandated by the Individuals with Disabilities Education Act (IDEA). At that time, no one shared with me the basic rights I have as a parent in the special education system. No one told me what services are appropriate for my child. All the materials they sent me were in English. How could I do anything? No one told me I could have access to a professional interpreter at IEP meetings and written materials translated into my native language.

These experiences forced me to change my way of thinking about disability and special education: I cannot just sit and wait for the teacher to do the best for my child. I have to get involved. Back in my country, people with disabilities are considered dependent and unproductive. I learned that IDEA protects parents of children in special education, that parents have rights of which they should be informed. Parents need to voice their concerns and collaborate with school personnel to best support their children. I believe in the power of sharing. I know that Tiny has lots of potential and will be successful in life as long as I build relationships with professionals who together uncover her strengths. My vocabulary reservoir is now filled with novel terms: self-determination, self-advocacy, person-centered planning, transition, vision, independent living, community belonging, and integrated employment.

STUDENT REFLECTION: I learned that children with disabilities, especially from immigrant families and families of color, are often neglected in the education and health fields, and their families face a lot of prejudice and lack of understanding of the system. What stood out was how much these parents have to face in order to advocate for their children. —Graduate student

---

LEARNING TO ADVOCATE

Questioning and speaking up to school personnel was a new concept for me. In Vietnam we are taught to respect teachers and others in authority. Parents are expected to provide food and shelter so their children have enough energy to learn at school, and then help with homework at night. Parent engagement is very different here in the United States. During Tiny's first year in public school, I seldom contacted the teacher or asked questions, thinking they would do what was best for her. Every time I was invited to a school meeting I worried that Tiny might have violated school rules or that I was going to be scolded. Since Tiny had no educational experience prior to coming to the United States, I was thankful she had an opportunity to go to school and participate in many different activities, just like any other typical kids. Because of this, I did not question the team when they praised Tiny's tremendous progress, saying she made so many friends and learned different skills, even though I did not see these gains at home.

STUDENT REFLECTION: While working in a school system last year that was comprised of mainly Vietnamese- and Spanish-speaking families, I saw firsthand how staff and teachers in a school can misconstrue lack of family involvement in IEP meetings as "not caring." The first takeaway I have from this experience is that just because a family is not incredibly verbal or pushy in an IEP meeting does not mean that they do not care for their child or about getting services for that child. It can likely be a scary and over-whelming experience for people who do not fully understand the system or language. —Graduate student

Over time, I learned that parents have to not only communicate and collaborate with school personnel, but also be fully engaged in the process in order to make informed decisions about their children's needs and services. Here, parents play an equal decisionmaking role. However, there was so much to learn to fully engage as a parent. Concepts such as inclusion, independent living, self-determination, self-advocacy, integrated employment, guardianship, and special needs trusts are novel to the Vietnamese community and do not have direct translations in Vietnamese. Advocacy is not just a matter of learning English or using interpreters, but understanding new concepts, incorporating them within the context of their child's IEP, and navigating cultural conflicts with them.

I still struggle with balancing my cultural values while searching for services for Tiny. I do not have a support network of extended family members here, as I would if I were still in Vietnam. I thought, here in the United States, if you do not speak the language and you do not assimilate into the mainstream, you will be forgotten. You can continue on this path all alone, and nobody will help unless you break a basic cultural value and reach out for help. Culturally, for me, I am assimilating. I am trying to change my own cultural thinking.

After my first experience in an IEP meeting when the SLP said to stop speaking Vietnamese to Tiny, I realized I needed to step up and help Tiny and other Vietnamese parents who have children with disabilities. I always found somebody to go with me to IEP meetings because it was so challenging to be there alone with my limited English, trying to make decisions about services and interventions. I felt a huge change in the atmosphere in subsequent IEP meetings when I brought in a friend with me to the meeting who looked like all the team members. I also noticed a significant change when an educational advocate was present. I wish the team members spent time building a relationship with me, as the parent, back then. I wish they respected my different cultural values, which have a real impact on how I approach and understand special education. Both parents and educators share a common goal of supporting our children's outcomes, and we need to work together to remove the system barriers and gain equity for all children, including Tiny.

THE POWER OF DAILY COMMUNICATION
BETWEEN HOME AND SCHOOL

I am supposed to be an equal member of Tiny's educational team, but many times, it is just one-way communication. I used to write a note to the teacher every day, but I never got a response back. I did not even know if the teacher ever read the note. I hardly knew what my child did at school and what I could carry on at home. All I received were calls from the principal asking me to pick up Tiny for her behaviors, for being injured by other kids, and for not feeling well. I could not even call the team back other than leaving a voice message on a phone machine, waiting in vain for someone to call back. I kept my notebook with my daily note to the teacher, but sadly, only one or two notes were entered by her teacher. I eventually created a visual schedule so that her teacher could check off what classes Tiny had at school that day. It was limited information, but at least it helped me visualize what her day looked like.

I then learned from my friends, also the parents of a child with a disability in the district, that if something is not in the IEP, it is not happening. From that day on, I learned how to document everything (e.g., Tiny's progress, conversations with school personnel) as much as possible in order to have evidence when communicating with the team. Tiny cannot tell me about her school day—whether she had a good or a bad day, whether she likes her food at school, whether she is bullied—so I demanded weekly communication in order to be informed and incorporate this into her day across settings.

Even now, I always start my day by writing a brief note to Tiny's teacher to share what we did the night before to help the team communicate with her. I include information like, "Tiny had a birthday party with her peers and a lot of sugar, so she could be tired at school"; "Tiny's period started, so she could be cranky and not fully herself"; or "Tiny just came back from her trip, so it may take some time for her to get back to more structured activities." I hope this information helps her teachers to better support her, especially if she looks or behaves differently that day. Teachers now write things back to me like "Today Tiny went to the bank to cash her check, and the grocery store to buy her favorite snack"; and "Today Tiny's favorite teacher was out, so she did not want to participate in many school activities." This explains how Tiny behaved at school and provides information so I can facilitate a real conversation with her and verify what she tells me. Collaboration is key, and many times kids behave very differently in different settings. The more parents and school staff communicate, the better we support our children. It reduces miscommunication and increases consistency in teaching Tiny skills to function independently.

Though I set this expectation for the last 10 years, and it is written on the IEP, I still have to reinforce the importance of home–school communication every year. Some teachers are willing to share the information, and some might not be. Some might be very detailed, and some might just write one sentence or write once a week. I wish I did not have to continue to fight for this and that my daughter could tell me what is going on at school, what her school day is like, and what friends she has.

A VOICE FOR MY DAUGHTER

It is all about communication with Tiny. School engagement, social interactions, and community participation all depend on her ability to convey her thoughts and desires. Not having access to a consistent means of communication leads to

Photo 3.3. Tiny as a Toddler Using the Computer at Home to Learn Communication and Literacy

behaviors the school views as challenging. I constantly stress to others that though she is nonverbal, that does not mean she has nothing to say (see Photo 3.3).

The very first system of communication Tiny learned was American Sign Language. However, she has trouble with fine motor control due to her low muscle tone from one of her chromosome disorders, so she created her own signs that were not universal. Scratching her forehead on the right side meant she wants to go to Target. She also had her own signs for her favorite fast food restaurants, KFC and McDonald's. Only those who knew her well could understand what she meant. We used DVDs to practice, and I tried to find accommodations for her physical limitations. Then we switched to Picture Exchange Communication Systems (PECS), which is universal and more easily understood. Unfortunately, the album of PECS symbols became too heavy to transport, and it also became limiting in her vocabulary and sentence structure.

To keep up with Tiny's vocabulary and literacy development, I explored high-tech options for augmentative alternative communication (AAC). The SLP at Boston Children's Hospital introduced me to an iPod with Proloquo2Go (a symbol-based AAC app). I spent endless hours teaching myself the app in order to teach Tiny. She is a fast learner, so she quickly figured out how to access her favorite music on this device, which she did often! Therefore, we needed to update to another system. I also used to give her the iPod to hold her attention while we drove places, but she developed a habit of throwing the iPod out the window of the moving car. Once, a friend and I went back to the highway to try to find the iPod in the dark. I wish that was on video; it would look so funny to passersby! Luckily, several friends donated their older iPods to Tiny at that time.

Together with the SLPs at the clinic and school, we explored a dedicated speech-generating device called Dynavox Xpress. She could read books using this device and could communicate her basic needs and wants with me. The challenge with this device was the complexity of programming that required an SLP trained in AAC to individualize vocabulary for Tiny. It also weighed a lot, so after 2 years, I switched to her current device: an iPad with an app called TouchChat HD–AAC with WordPower™ (see Photo 3.4). The iPad is more portable and durable, and it has universal appeal. Tiny does not stand out among her peers with this device because many students use iPads. I am exploring Real Vocal ID, which would

Photo 3.4. Tiny Asking Her Teacher to Take Her to Best Buy Using TouchChat HD with WordPower™ on an iPad

allow a voice that matches her age, gender, personality, and ethnicity instead of the computerized voice.

I found it was critical to use Tiny's strengths and interests to encourage communication development. When she showed great interest in balloon animals, I taught myself to be a balloon twister so that every morning she could communicate more with me by requesting what animal she wanted (see Photo 3.5). She would get her talker (i.e., her iPad with TouchChat WordPower) and say, "I want dolphin balloon," or "I want monkey balloon." This also helped her walk down to the bus stop, as she carried her balloon animal on the school van. Over time, she expanded her language by adding color and other details, such as, "Mom, I want a red snail with black antennas, please."

After balloon animals, she collected Pop Toys, a kind of bobble head doll corresponding to movie characters (see Photo 3.6). This interest allowed us to expand her language even more through watching movies, understanding different characters, and collecting her favorites. Her very first Pop Toy was Gamora from *Guardians of the Galaxy* (a green girl with pink hair). Every time Tiny went to a fair, her choice for face painting was without doubt, "Gamora pop toy." When the artists told her they did not know how to draw this character, Tiny asked them to look it up on their phones. She now has a large collection of these, and we expanded her language by identifying stores and locations where we could find them.

Photo 3.5. Tiny with Her Balloon Flower Bouquet That I Twisted on Her 12th Birthday

Photo 3.6. Tiny
Is So Happy
Receiving Her
New Pop Toy

Tiny now has a great interest in emojis and reads Emojipedia to understand the meaning of each one she finds. She can tell you the meaning of each emoji and filter through the different skin colors. Tiny has been focused on the pregnant woman emoji for a long time. With that, I have taught her the process of having a baby. I hope to be able to use this to teach her about privacy, healthy sex, and safety. Not all parents of people with disabilities are comfortable talking about these sensitive topics. Still, it is important to help keep our children safe in the world.

As one might imagine, it was not an easy task being a single mom, working full time, exploring the communication options, programming Tiny's devices, and practicing on a daily basis with Tiny so she could have access to her voice. However, I had no choice because school personnel perceived her as less academically skilled than I know she is, and they did not view her as capable of communication. Some years, the school had no communication goals in her IEP. Even when they did, Tiny did not always have her device with her, as if some parts of the school day did not require communication! School personnel rarely programmed context-specific language into her device, limiting her communication to general words and phrases in those places (such as art and lunch). I had to do much of this AAC work myself. I taught her at home, kept detailed weekly logs of her usage rates and language, and videotaped all of it. I showed videos and data at meetings to convince them of her sophisticated communication skills and potential as a learner.

FIGHTING FOR APPROPRIATE SERVICES

I am Buddhist, which is influenced by Confucian principles from China. So education is key for us. We always want kids to be successful, and advanced education is something we consider a tool to help us have a better life. I am always teaching and helping Tiny so she can reach her potential. In the Vision Statement from an early IEP, I described my goals as follows:

> Tiny is a child who is prompt dependent, and I want her to be more independent as well as expand her expression, understanding, and skills for living and learning through challenging goals and benchmarks. We envision that her school program will have the staff expertise to support Tiny in all environments and work with her at the same level of performance as we see at home. We envision that Tiny will be more independent and show us more of who she truly is and what she is capable of achieving with the appropriate teaching, support, and program.

Despite these expectations, most school professionals do not see beyond her behaviors. For example, in the same IEP, the entire description of how Tiny's disabilities affect her progress in the curriculum is just three short sentences: "[Tiny's] disability affects progress in all areas. She displays limited nonverbal communication skills and understanding of language. Attentional and behavioral issues affect completion of all tasks." Further, Tiny had a 1:1 paraprofessional, largely due to perceptions of her behaviors as uncommunicative and challenging. Unfortunately, this aide was constantly by her side and did everything for her. At the meeting, they would tell me, "Tiny did so many great, different things," but I never saw evidence of these things at home.

I think back to another early IEP meeting when I was trying to work with the SLP to learn sign language so I could integrate it at home because I had no means of communicating with Tiny, and she was challenging in terms of her behaviors. I asked her to show me what to do. The SLP stared at me and said, indignantly, "When you want to learn to do speech therapies at home, guess what? I spent 4 years to become a speech pathologist, and now you want me to teach you so that you can become a speech pathologist?" It was clear she would not help me. I had no idea what I should do. I just sat there at the IEP meeting and cried. I only wanted to learn something to help my child.

Following frustrations like this, I advocated for changes. The district placed Tiny at a different elementary school, one that utilized applied behavior analysis interventions. There were two problems at this school. First, manners are key in my culture. I wanted Tiny to use *please* and *thank you*, but the school professionals ignored my requests to work on this with Tiny. Second, the teachers and paraprofessional repeatedly asked Tiny the same questions during lessons, and they were questions she could answer! For example, "What is your name?" They knew her name, and she knew this, so why should she be motivated to tell them every day? Tiny got bored doing the same things repeatedly, which led to negative behaviors. Why didn't they arrange an authentic learning situation in which she could meet a new person who could ask her to share her name?

STUDENT REFLECTION: Hearing about Tiny's educational journey has made it clear to me that, with the right resources, the U.S. special education system can provide an appropriate education in the best interest of every child. However, it is also clear that the only way this system can be effective for students like Tiny is with a parent taking on the immense responsibility for navigating the system and often battling with school personnel for services. —Graduate student

---

Over the course of a couple of years, I engaged in the dispute resolution process of mediation twice. The first was to add communication goals and services in the IEP, and the second, to request a more appropriate educational placement for Tiny. The school brought in an attorney at both of these mediations and onward. The second mediation led to her placement in her third and current school, a nationally known private school for children with autism. I appreciate the new school's focus on physical, emotional, and intellectual development, unlike the prior school's emphasis on behavioral interventions. Here I finally have consistent communication with school personnel about Tiny's progress through a daily communication log.

However, while they are receptive to communication goals and services in the IEP, not all teachers are on board with it. The SLP works well with Tiny, but the SLP cannot be the only one responsible. I also worry about social consequences resulting from Tiny not spending enough time with typically developing peers. Additionally, I am not sure why the district continues to keep an attorney on my case. It is truly intimidating to attend every IEP in the presence of the school attorney. Just like school personnel, I want my daughter to be successful while also being mindful of limited resources. Why don't we use that budget to build a stronger program for more children with disabilities?

STUDENT REFLECTION: When I heard that Oanh had to go through mediation twice because the first resulted in no change in services, I just felt depressed. I knew that the system isn't always perfect, but when the people responsible for helping families are the ones who refuse to support, I just don't understand. —Graduate student in Special Education

---

ENGAGING AS A CULTURAL BROKER

Because I could find no support for Vietnamese parents when I was first looking for help, I established a support group for Vietnamese parents of children with disabilities, called the Vòng Tay Cha Mẹ Việt (Circle of Vietnamese Parents). Armed with my personal and professional cultural experiences, and my newly gained knowledge of U.S. disability service systems, I became a *culture broker*: a connector and negotiator between the Vietnamese immigrant community and the system of social supports available to them here in Boston.

After completing my second master's degree when Tiny was 7 years old and starting the Circle of Vietnamese Parents support group when Tiny was 9 years old, I started working for the same Parent Training and Information Center (PTI) that I turned to for educational advocacy and empowerment when Tiny was younger. My colleagues and I at the PTI address language access issues by engaging as culture brokers to educate families about the different systems of support and, at the same time, educate those who work (or will work) with families about culturally different values that might impact their service access. From the trust and relationships we have with culturally and linguistically diverse (CLD) families, we supported a few CLD parents to provide both verbal and written testimony on the importance of having certified interpreters and translators in the special education system. Although some translated documents are available on state disability websites, they are often not helpful due to the poor quality of translation or because it was not translated in the context of disability. The interpreters that schools provide might not have a good understanding of special education and can be counterproductive in helping parents. For example, at one IEP meeting, school personnel informed parents from my group that their child would receive "*accommodations*" at school. The interpreter translated that their child would be provided with "*hotel and food.*" The parents were so confused that they did not want to send their child back to school for fear that their child would be locked in a hotel.

In addition, I have hosted many public events, including an annual Tet/Lunar New Year celebration for hundreds of Vietnamese families (see Photo 3.7), monthly support groups for Vietnamese families with children with disabilities, and successful fundraisers. I have collaborated with the authors (Janet and Zach) on presentations at local, regional, and national conferences.

Photo 3.7. Tiny and Me in Our Traditional Dress at the Tet Celebration

Photo credit: André Ruesch

DIFFERING VIEWS OF TINY

The following poem was written by a graduate student after Oanh presented in the second author's (Zach) class.

A beautiful baby girl, born in Vietnam,
    To Oanh, a mother dedicated to her small child.
    Nothing wrong with an infant so tiny.
Her name is Tiny.

A few years pass by, but Tiny doesn't speak.
(Why doesn't she speak?)
"She's just slower than the other children," they said.
    "She will catch up," they said.
A diagnosis of "she's fine" and an instruction to keep going.

But a mother's intuition takes her across the world—
In America she discovers the words her own doctors couldn't find. Tiny has
    autism, a diagnosis in need of knowing.
A mother finds support she couldn't find back home.
The support comes with complications, none alone.
She encounters low expectations and preconceived notions of Tiny's ability to
    succeed.
Constant battles with educators who don't understand the importance of saying
    "thank you" and "please."
A speech pathologist dedicated to denying her the ability
To exchange signs with her daughter.
It would make more sense if these resources were in order.
Tiny is smart, she simply communicates differently.
Videos finally prove Tiny and her ability.
In all of this effort
Oanh fought the system
Attended IEP meetings until she worked with them—
Found her way to a school
Where Tiny was accepted.
Her needs were specialized,
Their techniques were inclusive.
And all the while,
Tiny has been a child.
Just because she doesn't speak
Doesn't mean she doesn't have
Anything to say.
She's just an 11-year-old girl—
Finding her own way.

Tiny is a lovely young woman, and she is very social. Sometimes people do not realize this. People new to Tiny should not "freak out" if she sits on your lap and rubs her forearm on your nose, because it is a sign of affection. She loves the iPhone, especially watching videos with Sailor Moon, a Japanese character. Tiny is motivated by earning time on the iPhone.

Tiny communicates in both Vietnamese and English using her iPad. Though it was difficult to do, I am so pleased that I did not comply with that SLP years ago who discouraged me from teaching her Vietnamese because Tiny is now bilingual. Tiny's communication skills keep her connected to family. Thanks to technology, we stay in touch with my family back in Vietnam. My mother does not speak English, so in order for her to communicate with Tiny, either my siblings or my nieces or nephew have to be present in order to translate. Tiny understands both English and Vietnamese, so she can respond in English to what her grandma asked in Vietnamese, as her talker does not have Vietnamese on it. Vietnamese is not yet available for any AAC systems. I can program Vietnamese on her talker using the phonetic spelling, but it takes a lot of time.

In one of the many videos I still record of Tiny using her iPad, Tiny says she loves books, Asian catalogs, swimming, the Zooble game, and frozen yogurt (see Photo 3.8). She LOVES to read! She loves to have me read books to her and she loves reading books herself. However, she would never like to reread any book. When I go to the library to check out a book, if she has already read the book, she will not want to check it out again. She throws it in the pile to say, "I read that, I don't want it again." It is just amazing to see how strong Tiny's memory is.

I am still sometimes frustrated because school personnel fail to fully appreciate that Tiny is a complete human being with strengths, interests, and untapped potential in addition to her needs and challenges, which are more apparent at first glance—and

**Photo 3.8. Tiny
Reading a Toy
Catalogue**

especially if you are looking for them! In formal special education documents, a deficit orientation persists. In Tiny's current IEP, the "Student Strengths and Key Evaluation Results Summary" consists of a bulleted list using clinical terms to describe her needs, followed by a brief recognition of skills, and an ultimate emphasis of her deficits:

> Tiny demonstrates a relative strength in her ability to complete visual patterns and puzzles and to mentally organize information and object[s] in her mind. Overall, her nonverbal IQ score falls at the 10th percentile for her age. Both her receptive and expressive language skills remain substantially limited.

Despite this problem, I remain hopeful in the lifelong process of building trusting, culturally responsive relationships.

PARENTAL ROLES AND ONGOING LEARNING

Being a parent, I am confident I know about Tiny's strengths, interests, and the skills she needs to improve. Unfortunately, being a parent of a child with disabilities, I also play many different roles: special education teacher, speech–language pathologist, occupational therapist, and sensory diet specialist. With constant changes in my daughter's behaviors, I had no choice but to become a behavioral therapist to keep her safe. Many times I asked myself, "Why can't I just be a parent and enjoy every moment with my daughter as her parent?"

I am an advocate who still educates the public about her different ways of communicating. Tiny has a unique communication style; she has her own voice. Many times, people stared and gasped, "She is so rich that she has her daughter carry her iPad all the time," not appreciating that the iPad gives her a voice. Other times, people do not have the patience to communicate directly with Tiny. In a restaurant, for instance, waitstaff are in a hurry and look to me, imploring that I just order for her. But if I do, how is she ever going to become independent? She knows what she wants to order, but it just takes time to focus enough to find, select, and push each button in the correct order while processing her decision amidst the sensory and other competing stimuli in the room. I found a few autism-friendly restaurants where I take Tiny, and a few servers have enough patience to facilitate communication and take the order directly from her. That makes both of us happy.

Every stage of Tiny's life has brought a new learning curve for me. She missed out on early intervention services, which I wish she could have accessed. The journey from preschool to middle school included my education of IDEA and how to advocate. Tiny turned 16 in 2019. According to our special education regulations, the transition process starts at 14, and the team should help the student create a vision and attend the IEP meeting. Tiny has not had a chance to do this yet, and the team made choices for her that might not be what she wants.

The American educational system is built on individualism, choice, and equity for children with disabilities. However, these values may not align with the values and educational expectations of Asian parents like myself who grew up in Vietnam, where concepts of self-advocacy and self-determination are novel. Culturally, we believe that people with disabilities are dependent, and their parents will be responsible for their whole lives. It is considered abusive if parents expect their children with disabilities to work or to live independently. Parents are fearful that their children will be bullied, so they become protective and do not expose them to the community. I am not different from many other parents. However, I have been fortunate to work in the field and understand human dignity and rights. I will continue to change my mindset to expose Tiny to real-life experiences and teach her skills to self-advocate. It has taken quite a while for me to process this and explore ways to increase independence and self-determination for Tiny, but I know she needs to learn skills to function in life in case something happens to me. In the last 2 years, I have taught her how to text from her communication device, write emails, and call her favorite people, including her former teacher and therapist. Just like any teen, she wants to make and have friends. Thanks to technology, she can check her own weekly schedule. All this can help increase her independence. As the African proverb says, "If you give someone a fish, she can only have it for a day; but if you teach someone how to fish, she can have it for her lifetime." Thus it is crucial to collaborate with the school in teaching her the skills she needs to function independently in her daily life. Yes, it does take a village.

CONCLUSION

Looking back, I am now thankful to the very first speech pathologist who challenged me to think differently, to reflect on my cultural values, and to get out of my shy shell to advocate and collaborate with the team for appropriate supports for Tiny. It was this very first SLP who helped me embark on a tireless advocacy journey. I have explored special education laws, parental rights, and parent engagement, and built a collaborative relationship with Tiny's school team. She challenged me to overcome adversity as an immigrant, single mom who was new to the system. It has been an emotional battle. I share my journey with the hope that my fellow parents will be empowered to do the same and that educators will collaborate with parents to support the ultimate positive outcomes of our loved ones.

REFERENCES

Alperin, E., & Batalova, J. (2018). Vietnamese immigrants in the United States. Retrieved from www.migrationpolicy.org/article/vietnamese-immigrants-united-states-5

Bich, P. V. (1999). *The Vietnamese family in change: The case of the Red River Delta.* Richmond, Surrey, United Kingdom: Curzon Press.

Borton, L. (2000). Working in a Vietnamese voice. *Academic of Management Executive, 14(4),* 20–29.

REFLECTION QUESTIONS

- Oanh described examples at home and school in which Tiny performed in starkly different ways. For example, when asked her name (repeatedly) during lessons at school, Tiny did not respond. However, when speaking via video conference with her grandmother from Vietnam, she listened to her grandmother speak Vietnamese, switched to English for her response (because the AAC device did not have Vietnamese language available), and responded by typing on her AAC device. What accounts for such differences in what she is able to do? What does this convey about the nature of disability? What does this show about teaching?
- Within special education, IEPs (the document and the meetings) represent the intersection of policy and practice, and a critical opportunity for collaboration between families and school personnel. How would you characterize the interactions of Tiny's IEP team? What could be done to improve these interactions?
- Oanh shared the example of the speech pathologist who told her to stop speaking Vietnamese with Tiny in order to focus on English. What are some of the cultural norms, assumptions (about disability, culture, and language), and power dynamics at play during this encounter? How much did Oanh overcome in order to resist that recommendation?
- Why did Oanh work so hard to find Tiny a consistent means of augmentative alternative communication (AAC)? Despite successfully using AAC to communicate at home, Tiny encountered barriers to communication at school and in the community. What were some of the barriers? Based on Tiny's experiences with AAC, what are some best practice guidelines to ensure successful AAC use?
- Consider all that Oanh did to support Tiny to have an appropriate education (including learning how to twist balloons when she realized Tiny liked them!). Is it fair to expect Oanh (or other parents) to do so much? How can schools help reduce the pressure of this advocacy expectation on families?

Truong, T. D., Hallinger, P., & Sanga, K. (2017). Confucian values and school leadership in Vietnam: Exploring the influence of culture on principal decision making. *Educational Management Administration & Leadership, 45,* 77–100. doi:10.1177/1741143215607877

Vietnamese Ministry of Education. (2006). *Education and Training Reform Act No.24.* Retrieved from legislation.vic.gov.au/Domino/Web_Notes/LDMS/PubStatbook.nsf/f932 b66241ecf1b7ca256e92000e23be/575C47EA02890DA4CA25717000217213/$FILE /06-024a.pdf

CHAPTER 4

"Ella Me Apoyó"

A Latina Mother's Journey Through the Special Education System

Maureen Lothrop Magnan, with Janet Sauer

In a country with a turbulent history of policy and social treatment of immigrants, U.S. policies and practices regarding bilingual education continue to change. Perhaps surprising to some, Ohio was one of the first states to pass bilingual education laws, in the 1830s; in fact, several Midwestern states embraced European "ethnic schools" in which children were taught in languages such as German (Crawford, 1987). Changes in language instruction depended then, as now, on the political power of particular cultural groups. In a description of the history of bilingual education from the Colonial era to the late 1980s, Crawford (1987) examined the relationship between American wars and attitudes toward immigrants and language instruction. According to Crawford, following the American Revolution there was anti-English sentiment, but a sense of nativism following events like the Spanish–American War pushed for English as the language of instruction. He quotes President Theodore Roosevelt in 1907 lecturing immigrants who sought to identify themselves in ways that acknowledged their family cultural roots (e.g., Italian American) or who maintained their home language: "There is no room in this country for hyphenated Americanism. . . . Any man who comes here . . . must adopt the institutions of the United States, and, therefore, he must adopt the language which is now the native tongue of our people, no matter what the several strains in our blood may be. It would not be merely a misfortune, but a crime to perpetuate differences of language in this country" (Crawford, 1987, para 18).

Antibilingualism sentiments have resurfaced repeatedly. In a more recent article describing the changing attitudes, the authors note that the 1980s and 1990s were challenging times for bilingualism, perhaps in response to the 50% increase of English language learners in that time period (Fenn & Kenny, 2016). According to the Pew Research Center (Flores, 2017), while Hispanics accounted for only 6.5% of the U.S. population in 1980, by 2015 that percentage had increased to 17.6%. In some cases there is a stigma attached to immigrants (and their language), particularly if they come to this country without wealth. In other instances, there is confusion in the schools about just how to implement bilingual programs with limited resources, especially when families might have come from very different educational models or when a school might have families speaking many different languages. In spite of an increase in bi- and multilingualism, the push for English-only language instruction persists. There is no official American language, yet several states have declared English as their official language.

Complaints against bilingual education have persisted, but so have its defenders. In a 2018 commentary about the troubling history of English-only laws, Karla Molinar-Arvizo reminds readers, "Don't forget: The English language is an immigrant to this country, too." She refers to the value of the indigenous Navajo language for the Code Talkers and how they uniquely contributed to the success of World War II. In a special issue about immigrant students, David Nieto (2009) describes the history of bilingual education in the United States. He refers to Sonia Nieto, renowned scholar of language, literacy, and culture, who explains, "The United States is not only a nation of immigrants as seen in some idealized and romanticized past; it is also a living nation of immigrants even today" (Nieto, 2009, p.1). According to the 2010 census, for example, 22.2% of Massachusetts residents aged 5 and older live in homes where English is not the primary spoken language (Fenn & Kenny, 2016). After passing an English-only law in 2002, Massachusetts readopted bilingual education only to find itself short of qualified teachers (Torres, 2017).

AN ACT OF CULTURAL BROKERING

This chapter is the result of cultural brokering by Olga Lopez. Ms. Lopez was a certified special education teacher in Colombia for 15 years, and she directed a support program for families with children with disabilities. She describes herself as an immigrant and someone who currently works at the local Parent Training and Information Center as a cultural outreach broker with the Latinx community. She arrived in Massachusetts nearly twenty years ago with her husband, having left her home country because there was a lot of guerrilla fighting and they sought a "safe life." When speaking to a class of undergraduate students she says, rhetorically, "Maybe you know about that," in reference to the United States's anticommunist involvement in Colombia in the 1960s and the subsequent years of internal social conflict. Olga tells the preservice students, "I remember the 2nd day [after I arrived in the United States] my brother told me, 'You have to put everything you've done in Colombia in a suitcase and put it under your bed, because until you speak English here you are nothing.'"

STUDENT REFLECTION: Immigration status and experience can vary among different groups of Latinx people. A person or family who has the privilege of migrating with documentation and approval might interact a certain way with White culture. A person who has experienced traumas in their immigration and experience, and continuously fears deportation, might interact a different way with White culture. Similarly, a Latinx person whose lands were stolen from their families may interact differently with White culture. —Graduate student

She began her new life in the United States by cleaning houses and working in supermarkets. She took English classes offered through the Red Cross, then entered a community college, and later earned her second master's degree in special education. A few years later, a local public school hired her. Ms. Lopez describes working for 12 years in a variety of jobs and becoming a special education coordinator. Then, she explains, she left the public schools in part because she became frustrated hearing teachers complain about the students who were diagnosed with disabilities. More importantly, she left after witnessing a teacher humiliate an African American kindergarten girl: "It was so hard seeing the child . . . and nobody mentioned anything. The family never figured it out." Olga then described another particularly troubling situation in which she was asked to convince a Latinx family to sign paperwork that would end special education services for their child. She felt the school wanted her to do this not in the best interest of the child but simply to save money. These events led Olga to leave her career working in schools and begin working as a cultural broker to inform CLD families, particularly Spanish-speaking families, of their rights in the special education system. She strives to connect families to services, negotiate cross-cultural meaning-making between families and service providers, and educate service providers and other professionals about the needs of Latinx families of children with disabilities. She also connected us with María (a pseudonym).

"Four years ago, I met María," Olga tells my (Janet's) class. "She's bilingual and she's very well connected in the Central American immigrant community. María knows all about housing, food, and school support systems." Though María has an 18-year-old who was served in special education for attention-deficit/hyperactivity disorder (ADHD), Olga said María sought out her expertise to help her elementary school-age nephew who was diagnosed with autism. Olga and I tried several times to arrange for María to join my class and share her story directly with my students, but each time she canceled, once because her child was sick. I wondered if it was because of the increasingly hostile political climate toward immigrants.

THE EL SALVADORIAN–MEXICAN RESTAURANT

With the rain behind me (Maureen), I slipped through the door to the El Salvadorian–Mexican restaurant filled with the warm aroma of meat, tortillas, and vegetables. I recognized María, a mother of three sitting at a table near the door, and she greeted me with a smile. "Hola, María," I said, as I took off my drenched coat and sat down across from her. María had just come from a community activity where mothers get together to make things out of everyday materials that would normally be thrown away. Noticing my curiosity, María leaned across the table and swiped to a picture of one of the projects on her phone: pom-poms to put on top of winter hats. I immediately felt at ease with her friendly demeanor and gentle gaze as she explained how she likes to be involved in the community for the sake of her children. Perhaps this was part of the reason she agreed to meet with me to talk about her two children served by special education after having met me briefly only once before.

María and I first met at a parent leadership conference conducted in Spanish for Latinx parents of children with disabilities. The leader of the group, Olga, warmly invited me into the room as everyone helped themselves to bagels and empanadas and settled into tables around the room. Olga graciously gave me the opportunity to introduce myself and I explained that I was a Spanish teacher and doctoral student at Lesley University working on a project with my professor to help tell the story of parents with children with disabilities. As one of the only White women in the room, I was grateful for the nods, smiles, and the friendly "bienvenida" that welcomed me.

I took my seat among other mothers and community workers as a lawyer presented on how students who receive special education services transition to adulthood. While the lawyer introduced who directs the transition plan, she handed out a packet that provided a description of the Individuals with Disabilities Education Act (IDEA) and explained, "The state law does not explicitly address graduation requirements for students with Individualized Education Programs (IEPs), which has resulted in some confusion." She straightened as she picked up a pile of packets, saying she had to translate a few of them herself into Spanish and could not believe they were not already translated and available for families in all school districts across the state. The women around the room shook their heads in unison as the lawyer urged them to call the Department of Education and their districts to insist that all legal documents and IEPs be translated into Spanish to enable families to fully comprehend the laws and special education services their child may or may not be receiving. One woman near the back raised her hand and asked for the contact information for whom she should contact first. I found out later that this woman was María.

A FAILURE TO TRANSLATE

Although a few other mothers at the conference were interested in telling me their story, María, who had experienced the special education system with both her oldest and youngest sons, stood out to me when she expressed the importance of being a part of the solution in changing the special education system. I wanted to hear her story.

María is originally from El Salvador, where she worked as a teacher. She is a volunteer now and is in the process of renewing her El Salvadoran teaching credentials to see if she could possibly be an assistant in a U.S. school system. She was unsure about working as a teacher with her age and education background, but expressed that education is her passion.

María's 18-year-old son, Juan, entered the special education system upon changing schools when he was in the 2nd grade. He was evaluated at his new school, and the results revealed that his reading and math levels were similar to those of a kindergarten student. Juan was evaluated again by the special education program at his school and determined eligible for special education. At first, María thought things were going pretty well, not perfectly, from grades 2 to 5. Juan received speech and language support and attended the resource room for extra math help. María related that Juan continued to struggle to communicate the way he wanted to and explained that he "se frustraba porque él quería participar en el idioma" ["would get frustrated because he wanted to participate in the language"]. He was diagnosed with attention-deficit/hyperactivity disorder (ADHD), for which he was medicated. María seemed satisfied with the support he was receiving; however, it was soon time for him to transition to middle school.

María described the transition from elementary school to middle school as complete chaos. When it was time to have a team meeting to discuss his IEP, looking back, she realized that she did not understand her role in how she could support her son at home, nor did she understand her rights in the special education system. María had a basic working knowledge of English when she was called for a team meeting to discuss Juan's IEP. She did not, however, fully understand the significance of the IEP meeting for her son and herself, nor the special education process.

STUDENT REFLECTION: I wish that more parents knew they can have advocates, so they feel comfortable in knowing and asking for more services for their child. —Undergraduate student

---

Though Juan's school consisted of 78.8% Hispanic, 32% White, 1.6% Asian, and 7% Black students (according to the school district profiles), the documents María received were not translated. For her son's IEP meeting, María explained, a bilingual woman was grabbed at the last minute to be the interpreter.

STUDENT REFLECTION: Why wasn't the woman briefed or asked days in advance? It seems like the school team didn't think about the language barrier, yet it's so important to think about that in all scenarios. —Undergraduate student

---

The educators sat around the same side of the table together and one-by-one began explaining the update of their part of the IEP. The interpreter turned to María and asked, "Entendiste todo lo que dijo, ¿verdad?" ["You understood everything she said, right?"]. María did not. María explained that each time the evaluator, the psychologist, and various other educators talked and explained, the interpreter would just repeat, "¿Entendiste todo lo que dijo?" María asked, "What?" and the interpreter would repeat, "¿Entendiste todo lo que dijo?" without translating what was said. Telling me this story, María shook her head in disbelief. The interpreter did not translate the needed information for her to fully comprehend her son's IEP. Meanwhile, the team members assumed that the interpreter was explaining the IEP plan to María.

STUDENT REFLECTION: At a certain point, someone should've been suspicious if someone talked for 2 minutes, then the translator talked for 10 seconds. It would raise red flags for me about the content being provided to María. —Undergraduate student

---

Once it was clear to María that the interpreter was not going to translate the details of the meeting to her, she decided to venture into the conversation using her limited English. Upon hearing her speak English, the interpreter made eye contact with her, stood up, and left. The meeting continued with María struggling to communicate and understand the plan for her son, and she left feeling more anxious and confused. At the meeting's conclusion, the evaluator handed María Juan's IEP in English to look over, sign, and return to the school.

During the following days, María received phone calls from the school saying, "Sign the IEP. If you sign, your son will receive the services. Please sign as soon as possible." When she thought, "Sí, mi hijo va a recibir los servicios" ["Yes, my son is going to receive the services"], she signed the IEP. María then wondered "¿Pero qué he firmado allí?" ["But what have I signed there?"]. María described that the signature line was marked in green, as if that was the only important part of the IEP. With the IEP in English, María felt the language was just too technical for her to fully comprehend.

María's explanations accelerated as she told the story of this IEP team meeting and signing an IEP that she did not fully understand. Looking back, María expressed that Juan's IEPs did not include social and emotional goals, which she felt would have been the most helpful. Upon explaining how she signed the unfamiliar IEP document, María lowered her head repeating, "un caos" ["chaos"].

CHAOS ON AN IEP

María related that during grades 6, 7, and 8 Juan lived in this confusing IEP chaos in which he was not receiving the services or support that he needed to succeed in school: "No avanzaba en sus calificaciones, no quería ir a la escuela. Se sentía tonto, y más cuando tomaba la medicina" ["His grades did not advance; he did not want to go to school. He felt dumb, and even more so when he took his medicine (for ADHD)"]. María described what happened when it was time to meet again with the team as he entered grade 8: "En el octavo grado, me reunían y me decían, 'Tu hijo ya no necesita educación especial, no hay fondos.' Y yo, '¿qué?'" ["In 8th grade, they met with me to tell me, 'Your son no longer needs special education. There are no funds.' And me, 'What?'"]. When she processed that Juan would not receive the services he needed due to a lack of funds, she explained that it was as though they had given her a blow to the face.

María described that her son was having "problemas de comportamiento" ["behavioral problems"] at school. She believes that the problems generated from the trauma he felt in elementary school from being in a different level and classroom than his friends. She knew this did not justify his behavior in not following class rules. However, she wondered if things could have been different if his teachers had presented him with consequences instead of punishing him.

Following the last IEP meeting, the school told María that Juan would be put on a 504 plan: "Ni siquiera me dijeron qué era un plan 504. ¿Qué es un plan 504? ¿Qué es eso? ¿Qué significa?" ["They didn't even tell me what a 504 plan was. What is a 504 plan? What is that? What does it mean?"]. At 15 years old, Juan transitioned into high school on a 504 plan. María began searching 504 plans online and asking other parents to get an idea of what a 504 plan entailed. Furthermore, María is still angry that the record of his 504 plan was lost and not acknowledged by the new school: "No saben y eso, ay, me enojó tanto y este sistema escolar, ¿qué es? ¿Es un sistema escolar o qué? Es un desorden, una desorganización. . . . Esa escuela echó la culpa a la otra escuela" ["They don't know, and this, *ay*, made me so angry and the educational system, what is it? Is it a school system or what? It is a mess, disorganized. . . . This school put the blame on the other school"].

THE POWER OF WORDS

María arrived at Juan's school and demanded a plan by saying "necesito una reunión con un equipo" ["I need a meeting with the team"]. The school complied, and María was assigned a meeting with the special education director. María described her as "tan linda, que esa señora a mi hijo le quería tanto a ella. . . . Ella me apoyó, ella es tan linda persona, la respetan tanto" ["so lovely was this woman to my son, my son loved her so much. She supported me, she is such a lovely person, they respect her so much"]. María explained that Juan is anxious and restless due to his ADHD diagnosis. She described that sometimes people do not understand what someone else's situation is like, but when one puts themselves in the other person's shoes, one can understand that a person does not want to be restless or anxious, but instead, see it as a result of their condition. María smiled as she explained how

Juan described this woman: "Mi hijo dijo, 'Es una gran persona, es la única que me entiende. . . . En ese salón me siento bien. Ella me apoya y dice cosas como, ¿Dónde está mi Juan?' Le saluda, le saluda" ["My son said, 'She is a great person, she is the only one that understands me . . . in her room I feel good. She supports me and says things like, Where is my Juan?' She greets him, she greets him"]. When María met her, she felt the same about her. She said that she respected Juan and he respected her.

After María excitedly explained how much her son loved his special education teacher, I watched her smile disappear when she began to describe what happened at her son's first high school team meeting. When she entered the meeting, she noticed that one of the teachers was Latina just like herself. At first, María assumed she would be an ally for her son, but this quickly changed when the Latina teacher described her son as a *payaso* ["clown"]. María's expression saddened as she exclaimed, "Lo más terrible en la vida es cuando uno va y la persona en el equipo está de la misma raza, es latina, y quiere estar atormentándome, solo viendo lo negativo del muchacho" ["The worst thing in life is when one goes and the person on the team is of the same race, she's Latina, and wants to torment me, only seeing the negative of the boy"]. The Latina teacher had only negative things to say about Juan. María asked if she could focus on his strengths, but instead the teacher replied that he does not have anything positive. When she realized the teacher was incapable of identifying any strengths in her son, María shook her head and said, "Qué lástima. Yo dije yo estoy cansada de esta persona, ella era tan grosera" ["What a shame. I said that I was tired of this person. She was so rude"].

STUDENT REFLECTION: It should be always the positives first, and constantly talk about them because it's important for parents to know that their child is good! —Undergraduate student

---

NEGATIVE NAME-CALLING

During our conversation María appeared most offended when she mentioned the teacher calling her son a "clown" and stated that she made a complaint to the principal. She hoped for an apology, but instead the teacher replied, "Yo tengo muchos payasos aquí" ["I have a lot of clowns here"]. María explained that calling someone a clown in her culture is quite hurtful, and told the woman, "That is a funny way for your culture. You need to learn to respect us. That is not a funny way for us."

I asked María what Juan was really like, and her shoulders relaxed as she described him as caring, intelligent in his abilities, but tending to get angry when things do not go fairly. He has a job now. The school took away his opportunity to participate in sports, clubs, or after-school activities as a punishment for his behavior in class. She explained that this was one of her more challenging fights on how to better this situation for him. When he was behaving poorly in class, she said, instead of giving him opportunities to get better, "le quitan todo, todo, todo" ["they take it all away, all, all"]. It just created more worry for her son and for herself. Her son no longer wants to go to school.

"WE DEMAND THAT OUR CHILDREN RECEIVE THE SPECIAL EDUCATION SERVICES THEY NEED."

At this point in the interview, María paused and explained to me that she really does appreciate Juan's school and the teachers who work there. Her intention was not to make noise. She prefers to stay quiet. Thinking back, however, she wished she had rounded up the other parents, Latin American television channels, and other media to confront the school. Her intention was not to hurt anybody, but rather state on posters in front of the school: "Exigimos que nuestros niños reciban los servicios de la educación especial. Es un derecho. Con todo respeto, exigimos, por favor. Ya basta." ["We demand that our kids receive the services in special education. It is a right. With all due respect, we demand, please. Enough already"]. María shook her head saying, "Why didn't I do things like that? But I keep fighting and I keep learning."

CONTINUING TO LEARN, FIGHT, AND PUSH ONWARD

Juan has yet to graduate. He has a few more classes left, and María pushes him to get to school every day and tells him how it is so important to graduate to go forward in life. He claims that he does not like the environment in the school. He did not pass math and says, "No, mamá, no quiero ver la cara de esa señora" ["No, mom, I don't want to see the face of that woman"]. María sighed, "But here I am always fighting and pushing him to do better."

My favorite story María told me about her Juan was when he was about to turn 18. He came home and told her, "Mamá, cuando yo tengo 18 años, me voy a independizarme, me voy a ir de la casa. Ya estoy empezando a buscar trabajo. Tengo 2 amigos más que ya tenemos el plan de cuando cumplimos 18 años nos vámonos, fuera de casa a rentar un apartamento" ["Mom, when I turn 18, I am going to become independent. I am going to leave home. I am already trying to find a job. I have two more friends and we already have a plan that when we turn 18, we're leaving, leaving home to rent an apartment"]. Upon hearing this, María sat down with him and listened. She explained to me that she likes to be realistic and undramatic with her children even if it hurts. Therefore, she calmly sat down with him and stated, "Primero yo amo tanto a usted que sería una mentirosa si no te dijera que me dolería mucho si usted iría de casa" ["First, I love you so much, and I would be a liar if I didn't tell you that it would hurt me a lot if you left home"]. She then asked him if he knew how much the house costs every month and began to take out the receipts for clothes, shoes, Internet, and lights to show him all of the expenses she incurs each month. "¡Todo eso!" ["All that!"] her son exclaimed, but with a follow-up that he could do it all on his own. She ended the conversation with "OK, mi amor, cuando cumples 18 años, me dices para que te preparo tu maleta" ["OK, my love, when you turn 18, let me know so I can help you prepare your suitcase"].

One day, as his 18th birthday was approaching, he left a bit early before school had officially ended. While doing errands with her two younger sons, she saw Juan through a restaurant window sitting with two friends. When her sons saw the restaurant, they begged to go inside to get some chicken wings. At first, she was resistant, as it would cost money, but eventually she gave in and calmly walked up to greet Juan, who was seated with his two friends enjoying their meal: "Hola, mi amor. ¿Cómo estás?" ["Hello, my love. How are you?"]. She politely introduced herself to his friends and asked their names. Surprised to see his mother when he knew that he should have been in school, he attempted to explain that their teacher allowed them to leave early. She replied with, "Está bien, hijo, hablamos en casa. Me alegro conocerles (a los otros muchachitos)" ["It's all right, son, we will talk at home. I am glad to meet you (to the other boys)"]; and she headed home with her other two sons.

The next surprise came when her oldest arrived home that night. Calmly, María told him that it was not okay to leave school early. Her son agreed and then told her that his friends had decided to leave him out of their plan to move in together when they all turned 18. He explained how one of his friends wanted to leave his house because his mom insults him and treats him poorly. For example, she put his suitcase outside and told him to leave for not wanting to go to church one day. Juan said that when his friends saw how nice and calm María was to him and his friends, even with them skipping school, his friends refused to let him be a part of their plan to leave his mother's home. María smiled and replied, "Ah, qué bien" ["Oh, that's good"], maintaining her calm demeanor. However, the day he turned 18, María made sure to ask him where his luggage was for his move-out day, and he responded with, "Ay, mamá, vas a estar viejita conmigo" ["*Ay*, mom, you are going to get old with me"].

MARÍA'S YOUNGEST SON

María explained that her youngest son entered the special education system at 3 years old when he became involved in early intervention. He had an ear and speech condition. According to his doctor, he was not able to hear normally when he was born. Her specialist recommended the Head Start program for him, and from there, he went to kindergarten. She explained that the programs helped, and by kindergarten he began to speak. Her son was also determined to be eligible for special education and provided with an IEP in kindergarten, where she felt that the teachers were supportive: "El tipo de gente que está allí es tan amable y hay involucramiento de las familias. Está feliz con la escuela" ["The type of people there are so friendly and there is family involvement. He is happy with the school"]. María told this story with a smile, as she had already experienced the IEP process with Juan and felt that she had more knowledge and experience of how to navigate the IEP process with her youngest son. She explained that he was able to graduate off the IEP in elementary school.

STUDENT REFLECTION: I love how she has a better experience with her youngest son, and how they are supporting him. It shows how special education teachers and services affect how the student and parent feel about school. —Undergraduate student

---

FORMING PART OF THE SOLUTION

After María's experiences with Juan, she began to do her own research to learn as much as she could about special education. She told me we do not know it all, even if we are experts or professionals. She explained that every day is a learning process for us all and we need to stay current and just do it the best we can. When I asked her what she would change about the school system, she responded:

> Realmente donde la escuela necesita específicamente el apoyo que están dando a las familias en cuanto a la traducción, en los materiales en su propio idioma, no lo están haciendo. Lo mandan en inglés y tienes que pedir. Necesitan más maestros en la escuela que hablan el idioma. [Really, where the school specifically needs support is translating for families the materials in their own language; they aren't doing it. They send it home in English and you have to ask. They need more teachers in the school that speak the language.]

Research supports María's statements of needing materials translated into Spanish. Although the Civil Rights Act of 1964 states, "A failure to communicate effectively with immigrant parents is a violation of their civil rights, considered discrimination based on national origin," parents and sometimes even school personnel are not familiar with resources available to help manage language assistance (Mathewson, 2016). If a parent does not know how or where to advocate for translation, documents and letters may not be in the parent's native or preferred language. These language barriers keep parents from being able to engage as their children's advocates and be well informed about their children's progress (Mathewson, 2016).

María is also correct in pointing out the lack of Latinx teachers in schools across the country. With the growing Latinx population making up almost a quarter of the student population nationwide, only 8% of teachers in the United States are Latinx (Neil, 2018; Bauman, 2017). In addition, only 21 out of 100 Latinx students are going on to attend college (Irizarry & Donaldson, 2012; Monzo & Rueda, 2001; Ocasio, 2014; Ochoa, 2007). This disheartening academic outcome is likely connected to the lack of Latinx role-model educators, "who may be uniquely equipped to meet the needs of this group" (Ocasio, 2014, p. 244; see also Irizarry & Donaldson, 2012; Monzo & Rueda, 2001; Ochoa, 2007). When teachers honor a student's language and culture in academic settings, research suggests, this results in culturally responsive teaching and growth in Latinx students' learning (Matthews & López, 2018).

Locating and hiring more Latinx teachers in school systems to represent the growing student population, however, is challenging. Even school districts that offer bilingual education sometimes struggle to hire enough teachers for their growing Spanish-speaking populations (Fee, 2011). One promising approach is to recruit teachers from Spanish-speaking countries, providing them with the necessary personal, professional, and academic supports "to be able to relate to students and serve as role models on their journeys to success" (Fee, 2011, p. 390).

Although many of the challenges Latinx students face in academic achievement are often discussed in the literature, the areas of opportunity, strengths, and positive paths for Latinx students to become successful educators are not (Fee, 2011; Ocasio, 2014). Ocasio (2014) mentions that one of the keys to strengthening the pipeline for Latinx educators may begin with the 8% of Latinx teachers themselves; however, this group continues to be marginalized and does not yet have a strong voice in the literature.

Having interviewed and spent time with María on several occasions, I (Maureen) view her as one of the strong voices. In our meetings, she expressed her love for education, as she was an educator herself back in El Salvador. She said:

> Trabajé mucho en mi país . . . yo comprendo la necesidad de ser profesional, tener que apoyar a la gente. La educación es tan amplia y a veces tan negligente, hay cosas buenas, y yo valoro esto. No debemos enfocar en lo negativo. No vamos a decir que la escuela es malo, malo, malo. Claro que hay muchas cosas que fallan, y nosotros como familias tenemos que estar allí y formar parte de la solución. Tenemos deberes que debemos enseñar a nuestros hijos, que tenemos que contribuir. Soy voluntaria y ahora estoy en el proceso de renovar mi documentación de mi país . . . no me gustaría trabajar como maestra, por mi edad, quiero ser asistente, educación es mi pasión y me encanta. [I worked a lot in my country . . . I understand the necessity of being professional, to have to support the people. Education is so broad and sometimes so negligent. There are good things and I value this. We should not focus on the

negative. We aren't going to say that a school is bad, bad, bad. Of course, there are many things that fail, and we as families have to be there and form part of the solution. We have the duty and should teach our children, we have to contribute. I'm a volunteer and am in the process of renewing my documentation from my country. . . . I would not like to work as a teacher, at my age, I want to be an assistant. Education is my passion and I love it.]

As I listened, I wondered how difficult it would be for María to fulfill her dream of becoming a teaching assistant, or even a teacher, here in the United States.

MY OWN INTERFERING EXPERIENCES

This piece would be incomplete without including how my (Maureen's) interactions with María brought up experiences from my own life and how they affected my writing. First, María happened to live in the neighborhood where I had once conducted home visits and assessments with families during one of my first jobs as a caseworker for the Department of Children and Families (DCF). As I drove to the restaurant to meet María, I passed an apartment building flaking with paint and was bombarded with memories of visiting parents in the midst of severe monetary and domestic stress there. Before my career as a Spanish teacher and educational researcher, I provided services for children experiencing homelessness, foster care, abuse, and neglect. At the time, my caseload included primarily Spanish-speaking families, since I was one of the few Spanish speakers in the office. My job was to assess, evaluate, and conduct initial and ongoing case management of children and family services and needs. Upon reflection, I realize that my previous experience working with Spanish-speaking families and assessing family dynamics helped prepare me for my meetings with María.

Another personal connection related to María's experiences with the interpreter in her first IEP meeting. When María began to tell that story, my stomach dropped because I also was asked at the last minute to be an interpreter at team meetings more times than I can count. I remember one particular day when I was pulled in to help interpret for a Latinx mother and father in a special education meeting for their son. I had entered the meeting late and had no prior knowledge of the family culture or background when I introduced myself. After a few minutes of the meeting, I wanted to gauge how much English the parents understood and asked a similar question to María's interpreter: "¿Ustedes entienden?" ["Do you understand?]. The parents looked at me with blank stares and perhaps fear. I did my best to translate and communicate the information from the team members. However, the news I was translating dealt with their son's negative progress and behavior in class. I felt myself wanting to soften the interpretation, since I could see the pain in their eyes as they listened to how poorly their son was performing and behaving in school. When María told her story to me, I listened intently to how she felt about not understanding the technical educational jargon in the plan intended for her son and how scary that must have been. I saw these parents' faces in María's story. Without the language to help their children navigate the educational world, I knew I had left the parents for whom I interpreted feeling the same way.

CONNECTING THROUGH MOTHERHOOD

María showed me a photo of her and her three sons smiling. We looked at it together and she explained how the boys take care of her. I smiled, pointing out that she is the only woman in a family of four boys. She joked, saying the boys allowed her to be the *reina*, "queen of the family," and they are her *guardaespaldas,* "bodyguards." At the end of the interview, I showed her a picture of my own two younger children on my phone. We found ourselves sharing advice on what age to introduce a cell phone and how to reason with an adolescent about not knowing everything there is to know at age 14.

María and I left the cozy restaurant behind and started toward my car in the soggy street while we continued to laugh and exchange stories about our children. Despite coming from different countries, ethnicities, upbringings, and neighborhoods, we connected over our efforts trying to be the best mothers we could be for our children. María said:

> Pero yo siempre le digo a ellos que yo no soy perfecta, tengo mucho que hacer, pero ante de todo, trato de ser madre. Hasta mi esposo me dice que "yo sé que eres una excelente madre porque a la hora de la comida, primero sirves a los niños" y después a él a al final yo. [But I always tell them that I am not perfect, I have a lot to do, but before anything else, I try to be a mother. Even my husband tells me that "I know you are an excellent mother because at mealtime, first you serve the children," then him, and then finally myself.]

When it was time to depart, we talked a few minutes more by my car before we bid farewell. Then I climbed into my car with María's nurturing humor lingering in my smile. After having only briefly met María once before, I was grateful that she was able to share some of her story in the hope of becoming part of the solution.

REFLECTION QUESTIONS

- María suggests, "When one puts themselves in the other person's shoes, one can understand. . . . " Related to Juan, how might this change how his teachers view him? What are the implications of this strategy for how disability is perceived? What are the benefits for students with disabilities when their teachers and other educational professionals seek this understanding?
- One of the themes from this chapter is language access. Why is it important that María receive the IEP and related materials in her native and/or preferred language of Spanish? Why is it important that the school provide a professional language interpreter with knowledge of special education policy and practice during IEP meetings? What would these mandated accommodations allow María to do?
- How did María's experiences with Juan's special education services differ from those with her youngest son? What does this reveal about the nature of home–school collaboration in the special education system? What could school professionals have done to better support María when Juan was first diagnosed?
- María initially lacked knowledge of the special education process, yet she still possessed parenting, teaching, and advocacy skills in her cultural context. However, the structure and dynamics of those first IEP meetings for Juan prevented her full engagement. What were some of the barriers? What could school professionals have done differently to recognize and incorporate María's strengths and skills into Juan's IEP process?

REFERENCES

Bauman, K. (2017, August 28). School enrollment of the Hispanic population: Two decades of growth [Blog post]. U.S. Census Bureau. Retrieved from www.census.gov/newsroom/blogs/random-samplings/2017/08/school_enrollmentof.html

Crawford, J. (1987, April 1). Bilingual education traces its U.S. roots to the colonial era. *Education Week, 6*(27). Retrieved from www.edweek.org/ew/articles/1987/04/01/27early.h06.html?print=1

Fee, J. F. (2011). Latino immigrant and guest bilingual teachers: Overcoming personal, professional, and academic culture shock. *Urban Education, 46*(3), 390–407.

Fenn, B., & Kenny, K. (2016). Bilingual education never really left Massachusetts, but it's been changing. Retrieved from www.masslive.com/news/2016/09/bilingual_education_never_real.html

Flores, A. (2017, September 18). Facts on U.S. Latinos, 2015: Statistical portraits of His-panics in the United States. *Pew Research Center.* Retrieved from www.pewhispanic.org/2017/09/18/facts-on-u-s-latinos/

Irizarry, J., & Donaldson, M. (2012). Teach for America: The Latinization of U.S. schools and the critical shortage of Latino/a teachers. *American Educational Research Journal, 49*(1), 155–194.

Mathewson, T. G. (2016, July 2). Schools are under federal pressure to translate for immigrant parents. *The Hechinger Report: Divided We Learn.* hechingerreport.org/schools-federal-pressure-translate-immigrant-families

Matthews, J. S., & López, F. (2018). Speaking their language: The role of cultural content integration and heritage language for academic achievement among Latino children. *Contemporary Educational Psychology, 57,* 72–86. http://doi.org/10.1016/j.cedpsych.2018.01.005

Molinar-Arvizo, K. (2018, October 1). English-only laws have a disturbing history. Retrieved from www.newsday.com/opinion/commentary/english-only-laws-have-a-disturbing-history-1.21342273

Monzo, L. D., & Rueda, R. S. (2001). Professional roles, caring and scaffolds: Latino teachers' and paraeducators' interaction with Latino students. *American Journal of Education, 109,* 438–472.

Neil, E. (2018, March 13). Studies show lack of Latino teachers in the U.S. is a growing issue. *Al Día Education.* Retrieved from aldianews.com/articles/culture/education/studies-show-lack-latino-teachers-us-growing-issue/51982

Nieto, D. (2009). A brief history of bilingual education in the United States. *Perspectives on Urban Education, 6*(1), 61–72.

Ocasio, K. M. (2014). Nuestro camino: A review of literature surrounding the Latino teacher pipeline. *Journal of Latinos and Education, 13,* 224–261. https://doi.org/10.1080/15348431.2014.887467

Ochoa, G. L. (2007). *Learning from Latino teachers.* San Francisco, CA: Jossey-Bass.

Torres, B. V. (2017, November 22). As Massachusetts re-adopts bilingual education, teachers in short supply. *WGBH News.* Retrieved from www.wgbh.org/news/2017/11/22/local-news/massachusetts-re-adopts-bilingual-education-teachers-short-supply

CHAPTER 5

Mother Tongue

Sachin and His Indian American Family

Punita R. Arora, with Janet Sauer and Zach Rossetti

We begin with a fictional journal entry from Sachin's perspective written by a graduate student in special education after Punita, Sachin's mother, presented in my (Zach's) class about their family journey. It reflects one preservice teacher's work at reframing disability to identify Sachin's strengths and interests, understand his behavior beyond its surface appearance, and situate his needs in the context of his whole person.

WHO IS SACHIN?

Ba-dum-dum-bum. Ba-dum-dum-bum. Ba-dum-dum-bum.

The rhythm pours into my hands, bypassing all the things that make me uncomfortable. I've never practiced with these students before; we've never drummed together. Mother made me wear this shirt; it's uncomfortable, and she wouldn't let me change. I can tell that she's up to something. She won't tell me what she's doing, and I really hate surprises. But the rhythm, ba-dum-dum-bum, courses through me as if all these things didn't matter. It feels like the thrill of stroke after stroke in the pool, yearning for the finish. My brother is sitting beside me, and every so often he loses the rhythm, but me, I can do this in my sleep. It's one of the benefits of what I've got. The autism, the PDD-NOS, it gives me power over my music, over the tabla,[1] over the laps while I swim, and the history I learn. It keeps me focused and able to concentrate on what I care about. People don't understand the focus, they see me pacing or talking to myself, but that's only when the world becomes too much, and I want to focus back on what matters: on the music, on my thoughts, on what I'm here to do.

Autism is not always helpful. I don't like variation, and new experiences or changes can make me anxious. I used to experience the world in a medicated haze; it gave me the ability to speak, to learn, to read, and to communicate. But the haze is gone, and I'm still able to live my life and do what I need to do. I may not love social gatherings. I may not be the best conversationalist or the center of the party, but I have my friends, I have my family, and they understand me. They love me for who and what I am. I love sports like any 17-year-old kid. I wish I could speak Hindi; it would make being able to communicate with my family back in India easier, but I understand and can respond. I wish they hadn't limited me by telling my parents I couldn't do it.

I am a kid who has autism, not a freak meant to be shut up with a taped mouth and locked in a closet. I'm not an idiot who has to go back to school for the same things without any understanding of how much I've learned and progressed this year, even if that doesn't show up on your silly tests. My old school didn't get that. They didn't understand that autism isn't a death sentence or relegation to a second-class citizen. Now I can take honors biology and thrive. I go to classes with "normal" students, whatever that's supposed to mean. I can have my accomplishments valued and my uniqueness celebrated. I may not see many people who look like me in school, but I still feel like it's better than it could have been, than it was. As I continue to become an adult, there will still be challenges. My metric for independence may be a little different than for others, but I like my life, I like my family, and I like myself. What more could I ask for?

Ba-dum-dum-bum. Ba-dum-dum-bum. Ba-dum-dum-bum.

During the class presentation that inspired the university student's journal entry, Sachin's mother, Punita, played a video of her three sons (Sachin was about 17 years old at the time) playing the tabla at a New Year's gathering. She explained:

We just had our traditional New Year. I don't know how many of you may be familiar with the Hindu New Year of Diwali, but it's the Festival of Lights. Yesterday, one of the parents in their tabla lessons had this New Year party at her house. The tabla, you'll see, it's a two-handed drum, from North India . . . [video playing]. So, my son is the one in the red, and he's sitting next to his brother, just to his right. All of these kids take music lessons together, and their teacher is off to the side here. At any rate, we had a potluck dinner. And everybody was dressed up. Sachin didn't want to wear that shirt, but I said, "No, no. You have to wear that shirt." And he said, "No, I don't want to wear that shirt," and it was one of those things going on at home. And he had not practiced with this bunch of kids because we take lessons on a different evening, though he knows them.

The tabla is an oral tradition, so they don't read their music, they've memorized [it]. At any rate, he was really nervous. So, the teacher, over on the side, who doesn't appear in the video, had about a minute, and she said what it is that they're playing. So, her singing, the notation, or notes as it were, sound like "ta tadidikida ta didikida ta didikida." So, they hear it, and they play it. All of them are doing it. Sachin really does that well, and I think it's the disability that allows him to do that. He'll pick it up right away. But he played, and I think he played well.

The university students were enthralled by the tabla video, Sachin's artwork (which Punita shared; see book cover), and Punita's descriptions of their family journey. They honed in on her descriptions of Sachin as being more similar to his peers without disabilities than not. They learned more about Sachin. Punita continued:

He's really friendly. I almost wanted to invite him to come along today, but then talking about him would just put him—he would be beside himself and that would not be good. So, he's a really fun kid, he loves sports, he swims on the swim team. He actually got a medal in the summer swim program. He likes running track and field. He's got lots and lots of typical friends. He loves art. He loves photography. He loves art! And, this (shows colorful painting) was an art project at [high] school, abstract [art]. He got an A on that project, he's very proud of that, and after doing that, he kind of chills out in his room, and he'll take out a piece of blank paper and start drawing and coloring. So, that's another wonderful thing that has come up here after the move [here], is his interest in art.

A few years later, Sachin discussed his art with me (Janet). He was taking a summer drawing class at the local community college. Asked if he would be willing to let us include his artwork in this book, he said, "I'd be down for that." He showed me one of his sketchbooks and pictures of his artwork on his iPhone. He told me he does not title his work because each time he looks at it, a new interpretation and title come to mind. He added that he would not like to push his ideas onto the viewer. On another occasion, when he was signing the permission form to use his artwork in this book, there was a place for a title; this time he said we could title it "Dispositions." He explained that he often named his artwork based on songs or his favorite bands. He referred to English author Neil Richard MacKinnon Gaiman's work and said in one of Gaiman's master classes, he describes storytelling as "the opportunity to be God." Sachin likens the process of artmaking as his opportunity to be God. "As an artist," Sachin says, "you are meant to make connections; making connections through art is in a sense existential, philosophical, and personal." We discussed the cultural value of art and music. He recalled watching a video in a high school sociology class about portraiture and how people use art to see themselves. When asked how he would describe himself, Sachin replied, "People might have an opposing point of view, but I see myself as a flawed person doing the best he can."

Sachin's mother Punita says, "He speaks with an artist's sensibility, like a composer." When describing him to the preservice student teachers, she continued:

He got an academic award in biology last spring. The biology curriculum for him was adapted so he didn't have to do the full lab write-ups the way the typical students were doing. I think some of the writing was scaled back, but he did take the same exams, took the same quizzes, and generally I think the assignments were just slightly altered. So, the content mastery was there, it was just kind of, the volume of the material was just dialed back quite a bit for him.[2]

STUDENT REFLECTION: It truly struck me when Punita said, "He's just a regular kid. He just happens to have a disability." While I always thought I should recognize a child as a person first before recognizing his or her disability, hearing this statement from a parent who used only a few of the 45 minutes she spoke about her son to discuss his disability diagnosis completely changed this for me. —Graduate student

---

WHO IS SACHIN'S FAMILY?

My (Punita's) family lives in the middle of a very busy and loud intersection; we reside at the crossroads of disability and diversity (see Photo 5.1). My son's autism set me on a journey to map the distance between "disability" and "opportunity." It has taken me 18 of his 22 years to realize that the special education system (the System[3]) is as disabled as my son Sachin is affected by autism. Both pose unique challenges for students and families. I experienced how ill-equipped the System was early on in my son's education. Sachin was a chubby baby and a very tubby, energetic toddler (see Photo 5.2). He grew into a loud, curious, happy little boy who also had a very hot temper and did not transition well from one activity to the next. Quiet time was more of a goal than an accomplishment during those hectic early years. Sending my three sons off to school became a ritual that brought structure to life as much as school itself brought education to our boys. I only discovered the System's shortcomings when we learned of Sachin's autism and how

Photo 5.1. Arora Family at a Celebration in Kolkata, India, 2015

Photo 5.2. Sachin as a Baby

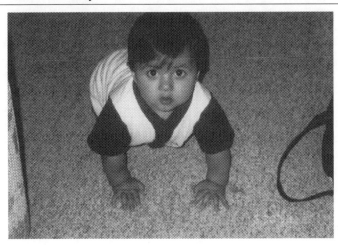

our cultural background was an impediment to Sachin's education. This is where my journey begins.

Sachin began preschool in 2000, right after his third birthday. I was thrilled to watch him take his first steps toward becoming a "big boy," just like his older brother, Rohan, who began school that year as a 2nd-grader. Sachin's younger brother, Manan, was at that time an energetic toddler who cried wanting to join Sachin. Mornings were complicated with breakfast, diapers, a stroller, and jackets to keep warm in Milwaukee, Wisconsin's fast-approaching cold. I was learning to be a more effective manager of time, multitasking my way through the blur of days and months that followed.

Sachin's preschool teachers recommended that we have him observed by school district professionals to help Sachin transition to junior kindergarten the following year. The teachers said Sachin engaged in parallel play and echolalic speech, and frequently had difficulty expressing himself with other children at school. I felt the sting of having my son singled out for observation and yet was eager and hopeful that they would see nothing "wrong" with him.

There were several tests and visits that year. One visit remains vivid in my mind. A friendly speech therapist came to our home to play with Sachin. I had prepared him in advance that a very nice woman was coming to play just with him, not with Manan. This was *his* special guest, and they were going to have a lot of fun playing with her cool toys and games. He was thrilled and greeted her at the door in a way that we had never seen before. I was hopeful that it would all go well for him and that she would just find him to be "a little slow."

That was not quite the case, as we learned at our first team conference in June of 2001. My husband, Ravi, and I attended the morning meeting, where we met all the early childhood experts who shared their recommendations for preparing Sachin for school. We learned that Sachin likely had PDD-NOS.[4] This was not a medical diagnosis; the team told us we would have to have our son assessed by a doctor. However, their findings were consistent with what that diagnosis might imply for Sachin.

We patiently listened as each expert shared his or her findings and recommendations, all of which resulted in a plan for the summer. The super-friendly speech therapist who seemed to adore my beautiful boy recommended that we not speak in Hindi with our children. She spoke glowingly of her time with our lovely boy, fondly recalling how excited he was to play with her and how she enjoyed her visit. However, that could not possibly take away our feeling of loss if we were to stop talking in Hindi. She insisted that this would be the only way Sachin would effectively acquire language skills, and the family would have to engage accordingly.

Ravi and I were crushed. We would have to cleave away from our Indian American children an essential aspect of their identity to provide for one son's success in school. All three paid a heavy price for losing their family's language. They missed a means to bridge cultural divides, even within a conversation, where English and Hindi may be spoken simultaneously. Our children lost their claim to a piece of their identity by not gaining Hindi language proficiency, which would have ensured a connection to their people, culture, and heritage. The System had framed our cultural ties as an impediment to education. We had to choose between family ties to extended families and the prospect for our disabled son's future success. We chose the latter. My children lost their access to their mother tongue (see Photo 5.3).

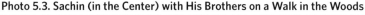

STUDENT REFLECTION: What stood out to me in Sachin and Punita's story was the fact that she felt part of Sachin's cultural identity had been stripped from him when the speech pathologist recommended [that] he not learn his native Hindi. —Graduate student

Photo 5.3. Sachin (in the Center) with His Brothers on a Walk in the Woods

CULTURAL CONTEXT

As with many countries whose history is complicated by a colonial past, India's independence from Britain led to lasting divisions. British history professor Sarah Ansari wrote about the controversial "Partition," the division of British India into the two separate states of India and Pakistan following World War II. She explains how Britain forced India into the conflict, and subsequently rushed into decisions based on dated maps and unclear motives that caused confusion and mass migration. Ansari (2017) wrote:

> Partition triggered riots, mass casualties, and a colossal wave of migration. Millions of people moved to what they hoped would be safer territory, with Muslims heading towards Pakistan, and Hindus and Sikhs in the direction of India. As many as 14–16 million people may have been eventually displaced, traveling on foot, in bullock carts and by train. Estimates of the death toll post-Partition range from 200,000 to two million. [See rare photos of this migration, "the largest movement of peoples in human history," at time.com/4421746/margaret-bourke-white-great-migration]

Ansari explains that identities were tied not only to religion, but also to territory, influencing some people's decisions to remain where they were. Conflicts between the newly established Pakistan and India developed and tensions persist today.

The National Portal of India (n.d.) asserts, "Culture plays an important role in the development of any nation. It represents a set of shared attitudes, values, goals, and practices. . . . A country as diverse as India is symbolized by the plurality of its culture." We might hear similar sentiments from Americans talking about our "great diversity," but there are differing perspectives on the advantages and challenges in any country's diversity (e.g., see Horowitz, 2019). Current demographic information indicates approximately 70% of India's 1.3 billion people identify ethnically as Indo-Aryan, and while the largest religious majority (80%) are Hindi, the languages spoken are much more diverse: 43.6% speak Hindi, but many people speak Bengali, Marathi, Telugu, Tami, Gujarati, Urdu, Kannada, and other languages (Central Intelligence Agency, n.d.). Although Hindi is the official language of India, even half a century after independence from Britain many Indians also speak English, and it is considered by many the "country's only lingua franca" (Masani, 2012). Their language proficiency in English undoubtedly influenced their status upon settling in the United States, where the Indian immigrant population has steadily increased since the Partition. In 2015 there were a record 2.4 million Indian immigrants living in the United States, making them the second-largest immigrant group after Mexicans (Zong & Batalova, 2017).

WHO IS PUNITA?

Like my own children, I too am the child of immigrant parents from India. I grew up speaking my parents' Gujarati, and my proficiency remains a source of pride for me and my family's uniquely American story. Most families from India, then and now, visit extended family in India every few years. Family trips to India provided me sweet memories of youthful family fun with cousins and elders, and explorations of beautiful, faraway places. My grasp of Gujarati, my parents' native language, helped smooth the bumpy years as I grew into a young woman.

My parents tussled with each other in defense of differing aspirations for their new life in America. My father left our ancestral home, a remote community in the western part of India, and came to the United States in 1958 to become a civil engineer. Like many immigrants, he came for an education, and the value of education has been a theme in my family. My mother was born to a wealthy family in Karachi, what was then part of greater India, prior to the Partition in 1947. She and my father had an arranged marriage between families and they eventually settled in Minneapolis. They often disagreed on what was required of their first-generation American-born young girls to succeed. My mom wanted me to feel confident and dignified, blending with my peers while reflecting Indian standards of feminine grace. She stressed politeness, good manners, carrying myself appropriately, and putting off dating until "later," when I would be "ready" (see Photo 5.4). My dad was more Draconian in his view. He saw no value for frivolous affect and wanted his three daughters to share his steadfast commitment to a perfect GPA, not getting distracted by friends, sports, and—most of all—boys. I did manage to have some fun during those years, despite it all, thanks to school friends. My compassionate and understanding mom creatively guided me through those fraught years, appealing as much to my head as my heart, as she imparted Indian values, tailoring them to our American context. She taught me to recognize how the world outside our home saw me as "different." I eventually learned to carve a place

Photo 5.4.
Punita, Age
13, on a
Family Trip
to Portage,
Wisconsin

for myself in school and college, building on shared values with others and embracing my identity, not hiding it. Our trips to India and my culturally complex home life helped me forge a uniquely American identity and express myself freely in whatever language I chose.

My Gujarati language proficiency allowed me to navigate culturally specific social situations and fostered a belief in myself. Oddly, our trips to India gave rise to a new identity as Americans, and Gujarati made that possible. To me, Gujarati is a living piece of what my parents left; it is a vital link to my family's telling of our story and is a mark of our uniqueness. Gujarati breathes life into my parents' memories of their lives lived *there*. It evokes the earth's fragrance, carried on warm and cool breezes, marking the sun's trek over life *in that place*. I thank my parents for sharing all of this with me through language. I show my gratitude in my love for the spoken and written word and more broadly for education itself. I hoped to become a professor of Indian history somewhere, delving into other stories about leaving, preserving, and becoming.

Nevertheless, my life took another turn, and parenthood supplanted my professional goals. Trying to help me adapt, my husband asked, "Well, what do you want out of this whole teaching experience?" I said, "If anything, I would like to just teach my students to value diversity among people." I have tried to impart what I received from my parents to my children by trying to teach them to speak in their family's language, for a connection to their heritage and family, and for confidence in forging their own identities. My husband and I hoped to visit family in India and to create new memories and opportunities for our boys. We share the belief that family trips imbibe identity and instill confidence in children. These are the moments to see similarities and stark differences. Most of all, they would learn to seek answers to their own questions about who they are in their own eyes and others' eyes. Family trips to India would teach our boys nuanced lessons to navigate difference and forge connections to shared identities (see Photo 5.5). Our choice to postpone these formative experiences affected our kids' tolerance for complexities. In many ways, their ticket to social acceptance and confidence was delayed, at best.

Photo 5.5. Sachin and His Brothers at the Airport in India, 2015

My husband and I struggled to explain our son's condition to family in India who longed to see us. What is the Hindi word for autism, anyway? It is *swalinta*, I eventually learned, meaning to be in oneself, an obscure word for an obscure affliction that was just "not normal." As his mother, I was and am blamed by some for this outcome. I feel their rejection of me in their dashed hopes, our absences, and growing absences in family pictures and timely words spoken.

We did not take frequent summer trips to India, as most Indian families do, to see family and familiarize our boys with their ancestral homeland. As a result, our kids missed out on learning to be comfortable in their own skin in the familiar and unfamiliar world that is India for those of us who grow up elsewhere. How would we even endure the long flight and manage jet lag and the usual water-borne illnesses? How would we explain our son's condition to family who could not grasp our limitations? We did not have words for unknowns about autism and therapeutic methods. How would we deal with the helplessness our other two boys would feel watching us squirm? This tension was in no part Sachin's fault, but instead involved the limitations of the social cultural complexities of the merging of cultures.

Something had to give.

We could not win on all fronts. Our kids eventually visited India later (see Photo 5.6). Their memories of India visits began in elementary school, when we first ventured onto an airplane together.

Travel to and from our home country helped our children form a new identity as Americans. This is counterintuitive. Ease and choice, competence and functional language proficiency allow for personal strength and confidence. Language proficiency and ease in culturally specific social situations remains a goal for many immigrants because skills connect to a place left behind in pursuit of life in America.

THE FAMILY AND THE SYSTEM

The System forced the decision on our family to stop talking in Hindi, or anything but English, thereby closing a path to language proficiency and cultural

Photo 5.6. Sachin with His Brothers in a Sacred Thread Ceremony in India

competence, in the name of academic success for a child with autism. The System made us comply with a broader agenda of assimilation, rather than supporting our family's values to retain our identity. It abandoned the greater good for our kids' classmates to embrace diversity and to understand the American immigrant experience as a part of what it means to be American.

Disability is a fact of life, not a social disease. The System relegated Sachin's autism and his diverse background as combined impediments to his success in school by devaluing our culture. The speech therapist's recommendation to stop speaking in Hindi and Gujarati at home represented a tremendous loss of a rich and meaningful life through language. We were effectively silenced because the System could not understand the importance of our value for our own tradition. Rather, it silenced our children, making them feel like outsiders in their own lives. To the world, our boys look Indian, but they cannot speak in Hindi or Gujarati and therefore cannot fully participate in their family's life without a language barrier or an accent to reveal their outsider status. I lost my ability to teach my boys to forge their own connections with my Indian-born husband's family. It is sad to me that we were told to choose between our cultural integrity and a promise for Sachin's success in school.

I wish that educators understood that language proficiency in one's mother tongue and comfort with multifaceted identities help achieve smoother transitions to life in America. Cultural and linguistic connections are a lifeline for immigrant students, especially those affected by disability. To sever these ties is to close the door on loving relationships, diminish fond memories, and relegate to the past something that can help in the present moment. A child's confidence in his own voice allows him to speak and not be spoken for. As Sachin's mother, I saw that the System relied on my compliance so it could speak for me and my family, ensuring that Sachin and our family would blend in with others at the cost of his individuality and our family's uniqueness. My husband, Ravi, and I wanted to impart to our boys the power of choice so they would feel comfortable in their own skin, confidently expressing themselves in a manner of their choosing. Instead, we decided to follow along as instructed to ensure Sachin's success in school. We mourned the conversations and exchanges never to be spoken and heard.

STUDENT REFLECTION: I plan to work in urban settings, and in many cases, these are the most culturally diverse schools. I want to understand what is important to a family and work that into my recommendations for the student. For example, I had many Spanish-speaking students last year, and even though they were in a bilingual class because their parents valued the Spanish language, students were chastised for using Spanish. I want to make sure this doesn't happen. —Graduate student

---

Life at the intersection of diversity and disability began in a quiet Milwaukee suburb. Then we moved to Indianapolis in early August 2001 for work, just before the start of school, only a few weeks before the 9/11 terrorist attacks. Though the boys would not have been aware of the impact of this event, to me it framed the

Photo 5.7. Sachin, in Kindergarten, Holding the American Flag

way in which I think other people reacted to our family. Even in mundane social interactions, I noticed people pausing, or looking at us differently. It is hard to explain. While I know African Americans, new to the neighborhood, would introduce themselves to the local police to avoid being pulled over, the attention we got was more subtle. Even in an area with a large Indian community, we overheard people questioning why immigrants, particularly people of color, move to America "if they don't like us." It was in this context that Sachin began Kindergarten, pictured here holding the American flag (see Photo 5.7). It brought up memories of our time studying in another Midwestern state when out in the community my husband was asked, "Are you from Iraq?" My family and I are accustomed to being misunderstood as members of an unpopular minority group.

Our 10 years in Indianapolis turned the noisy intersection of diversity and disability into an isolated purgatory of smoke and mirrors. We found an affluent suburb famous for its well-endowed school district so that Sachin would begin school with all of his therapies in place. We made an assumption that a well-funded school meant sophisticated services. We took our IEP that was developed in Milwaukee to Indianapolis only to learn that the wonderful things we were going to get in Milwaukee would not be available to us in the new school district. We were saddened to discover that there was no all-day junior kindergarten in our new school district and no music and art therapy, all services recommended in the IEP. Sachin was grouped in an early childhood classroom with students referred to as "low-functioning," who would join him in kindergarten the following year.

Sachin made progress. He began to speak (in English), learned his letters and numbers, socialized, and played with his peers. The school principal was probably the most important person in my son's school life during those early years. Mr. B.

was passionate about special education, inclusion, and equity. The teachers and staff in his school shared his vision to serve all students. He ended up taking an early retirement because of conflicts with the district's special education director. Mr. B. valued diversity in all its forms and was comfortable leading his school from a student-centered space, while honoring his budget and other mandates. The special education director was not known for kindness or creativity, and the school suffered after Mr. B. left.

Sachin's pediatric behavioral neurologist, who by that point oversaw a cocktail of drugs to address autism-related behaviors and tendencies, suggested that we enroll Sachin in a private school designed for students with autism spectrum disorders. The school was in a church whose pastor was a retired military officer. This place was a far cry from the beautiful school he attended in our neighborhood.

CHANGE OF SCHOOL, CHANGE OF SERVICES

Sachin had been ornery all day after coming home from school. My frustration gave way to anger after he said he finished his bath but appeared as dirty as ever, sweaty with black sticky stuff all over his mouth. He ran around the house, more energetic than usual, screaming back at me, "No, Mom! I took my shower already!" I brought him in front of a mirror and demanded to know why his face looked like that, and he said, "I told you already. Ms. Jackson put tape on my mouth and locked me in a closet at school! Why won't you believe me?" Terror and rage coursed through my veins like lava streaming down an angry mountain, cooled only by my teary sobs. I picked up the phone and called my friend Susan, who taught English down the hall from the closet in which Sachin was allegedly locked. She had her own two boys on the autism spectrum; our boys were good buddies, and I knew that I could call her for details about what Sachin just told me. Susan said that she did not hear anything, but she assured me that her classroom door is usually closed to prevent her students from getting distracted and that just because she did not hear anything did not mean that it did not happen.

My husband and I cleared our schedules for the day and met with Sachin's teacher, Ms. J., the next morning. We were shocked to have to explain to a school administrator that taping a child's mouth, binding him to a chair, and locking him in a closet is abuse. She sat patiently, looking us both in the eye, and listening to our concerns. She promised us that our son would never have to endure that kind of treatment again in her school. "But," she said, "other parents in this school don't mind our firm approach, and we'll continue to administer discipline as we see fit. Sachin will not be subject to our more robust measures, now that you've expressed your wishes." Disappointment and utter disgust would follow us through the remainder of the school year. Sadly, Ms. J.'s educational philosophy reflected the church pastor's command-and-control leadership style and reliance on corporal punishment. We could not understand how that church promoted the idea of Christian mercy as it facilitated the abuse and intimidation of children with disabilities. The adage "Spare the rod and spoil the child" seemed as much a motto as any Biblical instruction to be Christlike and compassionate toward children.

STUDENT REFLECTION: It is hard to imagine that there are still schools that treat children like Sachin so horribly. Although I do not need a reminder to not do these things, it is a reminder of the trust that parents and students put in their teacher. You are such an important role model for students and someone they should always trust. They should never fear you or feel they cannot confide in you. —Graduate student

---

My friend Susan and a growing number of parents paid close attention to the goings-on at school during that year. We volunteered to help with classroom duties and took the kids to another neighboring church's gymnasium for afternoon gym class. We chaperoned field trips, and we watched closely. Sadly, we saw Ms. J. regularly call the local Indianapolis police to come to school and threaten students with arrest if they would not fall in line.

Disgust morphed into nausea one day when we learned that Sachin witnessed Ms. J. paddling his friend Jeremy with a large wooden spoon. A teacher sent Jeremy to the office toward the end of the day because he was not paying attention. Sachin quietly followed him down the hall, without permission, when she turned to write on the board. He had a sense that something bad was about to happen to Jeremy. He stood outside Ms. J.'s office door and watched through the glass as Jeremy was made to drop his shorts and was beaten on his bottom. He wailed and cried in pain, while Sachin looked from outside the office, unbeknownst to Ms. J., who unflinchingly meted out her punishment for the common crime of late-afternoon distraction.

A few days later, I happened to meet Jeremy's mom when waiting to pick up Sachin after school and mentioned to her that I was disturbed about discipline at school. I did not want to make allegations based on what Sachin said that he saw. I instead shared what happened to Sachin in vague terms, knowing that her husband, Jeremy's dad, was a school district administrator in a town on the outskirts of the greater Indianapolis area. I assumed that they would want to know about such things, given his role in a public school district. Jeremy's mom did not bat an eye when she said, "That's why we chose this school over any other option. We gave Ms. J. a wooden kitchen spoon to whip him into shape!" She must have heard my jaw hit the floor as I gasped in horror at what she said in defense of her son's abuser. There were no words thereafter. I could only think about getting my son out of that hell. No longer would I serve my son on a platter to be destroyed in the name of teaching him to be a good person and contributing member of society. How could he learn to respect authority when those with authority could not see his humanity, hear his cries of pain, or understand his disability? Education seemed a distant goal in an environment where human rights could not be defended. We watched all this transpire over 2 years under one roof and within the walls of a church, of all places. The System failed him again. It seemed that we had no place to go.

Fortunately, Susan and another mom, Ruth, led a group of families to form another, wonderful school for our children. This school opened in the fall of 2008, inspired by Sachin's horror, with the aim of preventing that from happening because parents did not have a choice. Later, we moved to Massachusetts when Sachin was in high school.

Answering student questions in the second author's (Zach's) university class of preservice and inservice teachers, I explained why the move was so positive:

> I'm so grateful that we moved here to Massachusetts because it was just horrible in Indiana. It was horrible. . . . Well, his confidence level has just shot up, I mean, the school, I think, really appreciates who he is as a person. He is very energetic, exuberant, curious; he loves movies. If he does not know what to talk about, he will just automatically ask, "Oh, did you see this movie?" And he'll get you talking about the movies, and then you don't get to talk, he gets to talk. But that's a characteristic of autism, right?
>
> The music lessons are fantastic. They have helped a lot. Swimming, he is very good with swimming. He didn't do these things in Indiana. He had access to all this stuff, but I guess just something came together for him here in a way that he was able to take all this stuff and just make it his own. I don't know if that's a growth thing, or I don't know, but it's really quite remarkable.
>
> From my perspective, I feel that the teachers are very respectful and sensitive. I can tell that some teachers might be more "professorial," you know, more—you'll remember probably in your school career somebody who was just much more of a certain driven type of teacher. There is definitely more of that. In fact, one of those teachers is a coach in running and track and field, and you can kind of tell; I mean, Sachin is not the stellar, college-bound, uber-student, but he still is able to celebrate Sachin's successes. And I don't think I would have seen that in the past, at least where we came from, that that type of superb-caliber teachers would take an interest in a kid like my son.

STUDENT REFLECTION: I appreciated being able to hear Punita and Sachin's story. I love being able to put faces to an account, and speakers like Punita are incredibly helpful for someone like me, who has not had a ton of experience with families with disabilities. Although I hate to say it, part of me was intimidated to talk to families about disabilities and how they affect daily living. I attribute this to not growing up in an inclusive setting and not being socialized to look at something like ADD or autism as a "learning difference" like Punita put it. I value opportunities to talk to these family members because it opens up my eyes to look at disability not as a deficit, but just as a form of diversity. —Graduate student

---

CONCLUSION

I think that my son is typical in many ways of what you would expect of a 17-year-old autistic boy, but in many ways, he is not. If there is one thing that you take away from our story, let it be this: rather than depending on stereotypes of what you assume a person with a disability is like, *use generalizations to guide your questions.* You might ask me, "Oh, I hear that Indians eat a lot of spicy food. Is that true?" So there would be a stereotype of what a typical Indian mom at that event would look like—and I probably look like the typical Indian mom—but that is used as a segue to a question. Rather than a stereotype, which doesn't allow me the flexibility of climbing out of that little box that a stereotype is, general questions allow opportunities for growth through learning about people. There is a distinction between generalizations and stereotypes. Regarding students with disabilities and their families, it would be useful for teachers of students with disabilities to use those generalizations as a way to probe for more information from parents (and students).

I wish that I could go back in time to share my experiences with all those who shaped my family's life with autism thus far. I would go back to that first speech therapist in Milwaukee, when Sachin was only 3 years old. I would explain that her recommendation to stop speaking Hindi at home represents a forced perdition, a lobotomy of our identity and heritage. Sachin's resulting view of himself, first challenged by a diagnosis, would be further stunted by an assumption that cultural diversity somehow represents a "past" and not a joyful, vibrant "present." There is no such thing as "old world" and "new world" for families who live, love, and grow together over the Internet and through short jaunts on an airplane. Our language and ideas of becoming American must catch up with technology that bridges distances through the glow of blue light in a handheld device.

I wish that Sachin's formative years were spent with more teachers who saw his potential rather than his challenges. At times, we had great teachers because a school principal was committed to preserving and building inclusivity. But administrators cut him down. Then the community let us down by allowing for abusive policing. A doctor insisted that the abusive private school offered more and endorsed a substandard education model. The state would not improve access and quality for students with disabilities, but they were all too willing to tout the number of students accepted into Ivy League schools. Duplicitous attitudes hurt the most vulnerable among us; there is no virtue in inflicting pain on some just because they are different from the majority.

I wish that there were more school-based and community-based opportunities for my other two sons to feel understood and comforted for the unique challenges of having a sibling with a disability. Communities have a wonderful capacity to surround all children, and I wish my two typical sons belonged to special groups of friends who understood and supported one another.

In the time since my son's diagnosis, there has been a mushrooming of autism diagnoses. I wish that communities would recognize this fact of life and provide accessible, free resources to all families. A wonderful idea could be specific times to meet in parks, where families could plan to come and enjoy time together and meet others like them. This would also be great for families who belong to specific ethnic groups. They could plan to meet and enjoy speaking their own languages and meet others to share as a specific affiliation within the larger community.

REFLECTION QUESTIONS

- We hope that, like us, you were horrified by the abusive example Punita shared of Sachin being locked in the closet with his mouth taped shut. Yet restraint and seclusion remain active practices in schools across the country—often without state regulations for monitoring and reporting despite disproportionate usage with students with disabilities and students of color, and multiple deaths resulting from restraint and seclusion (e.g., see Abamu & Manning, 2019; U.S. Department of Education, 2013). Why do you think there is an overrepresentation of students with disabilities and students of color in restraint and seclusion practices? What assumptions or biases might be involved?

- How many languages do you speak and understand? Do you know the first language of your parents? Of your grandparents? How do you think having a shared language with elder and extended family might change your own relationships? Your identity? How could speaking multiple languages help you teach multilingual children and work with their families?

- Punita describes that she and her husband were "crushed" at the prospect of not speaking Hindi with Sachin and in their home. How does this loss affect not just Sachin, but their family unit and entire extended family? How might their lives have been different if the IEP team did not follow the speech therapist's suggestion? What are the long-term impacts of such a suggestion?

- Punita recommends that education professionals *use generalizations to guide questions* (e.g., about culturally diverse families or students with disabilities). She explains that not asking questions perpetuates stereotypes and assumptions about culture, race, ethnicity, or disability. Why does she recommend this? How have your experiences related to this suggestion? Can you think of a way to incorporate this into your own practice?

NOTES

1. The tabla is a traditional Indian percussion instrument that resembles a pair of drums.

2. Sachin graduated from his high school with a diploma that enabled him to take classes at the community college. Other students with developmental disabilities may not graduate with a diploma, thus limiting their opportunities for continuing education and related employment. For more information about access to higher education, see the Think College website (thinkcollege.net), and for more information about employment for people with disabilities, see Ross and Bateman (2015).

3. When capitalizing the S here, I want to emphasize the education establishment and the underlying expectations of families and students that are reflected in the policies and procedures.

4. PDD-NOS stands for Pervasive Developmental Disorder—Not Otherwise Specified. In the Diagnostic and Statistical Manual of Mental Disorders (DSM, 4th edition with text revision, 2000), it was one of five diagnoses within the broader category of Pervasive Developmental Disorders. Along with Autistic Disorder and Asperger's Disorder, it was commonly characterized as one of the three Autism Spectrum Disorders. Now, there is one diagnosis of Autism Spectrum Disorder in the DSM-5 (2013).

REFERENCES

Abamu, J., & Manning, R. (2019). Desperation and broken trust: When schools restrain students or lock them in rooms. Retrieved from www.npr.org/2019/06/05/726519409/desperation-and-broken-trust-when-schools-restrain-students-or-lock-them-in-room

Ansari, S. (2017). How the partition of India happened—and why its effects are still felt today. Retrieved from theconversation.com/how-the-partition-of-india-happened-and-why-its-effects-are-still-felt-today-81766

Central Intelligence Agency. (n.d.). World factbook. Retrieved from www.cia.gov/library/publications/resources/the-world-factbook/geos/in.htm

Horowitz, J. M. (2019). Americans see advantages and challenges in country's growing racial and ethnic diversity. Retrieved from www.pewsocialtrends.org/2019/05/08/americans-see-advantages-and-challenges-in-countrys-growing-racial-and-ethnic-diversity

Masani, Z. (2012). English or Hinglish—which will India choose? Retrieved from www.bbc.com/news/magazine-20500312

National Portal of India. (n.d.). Art & culture. Retrieved from www.india.gov.in/topics/art-culture

Ross, M., & Bateman, N. (2015, May 15). Disability rates among working-age adults are shaped by race, place, and education [Blog post]. Retrieved from www.brookings.edu/blog/the-avenue/2018/05/15/disability-rates-among-working-age-adults-are-shaped-by-race-place-and-education

U.S. Department of Education. (2013). Seclusion and restraints: States and territories summary. Retrieved from www2.ed.gov/policy/seclusion/seclusion-state-summary.html

Zong, J., & Batalova, J. (2017). Indian immigrants in the United States. Retrieved from www.migrationpolicy.org/article/indian-immigrants-united-states

CHAPTER 6

Lessons of Abundance in an Iranian-American Family

Kimiya Sohrab Maghzi[1]

Our Samin Banoo

Music and laughter are your delight;
The warmth of your smile,
Your compassion and empathy—
You are our light, our love, our teacher;
A well of inspiration.

My sister,
You nurture my soul!
Ice cream dates and
Family parties.
Khaleh Samin,
You are always so patient with my children.
I thank God I have you,
And you have me;
You make our lives more meaningful.

My eldest daughter,
I am so proud of you!
You are the answer to many questions
About the purpose of life
And what lies beyond.
You have taught me to detach from
This world's strifes;
You have become the heart of our growth.
My strong child,
My brave child,
You teach others without words.
Our beautiful Samin Banoo,

So full of happiness . . .
To be loved and have love . . .
Oh! The joy you bring to our family!
You soar in the realms of God
Because your spirit is limitless.

THE LIVED EXPERIENCE

We want to tell you a story about Samin Banoo, but her voice is silent in this narrative, as she has always been voiceless; she has no normative spoken language, although she communicates through unspoken emotion. For Samin, her family have always been her advocates.

This is also the story of Shirin, the mother of Samin, her second child. As an Iranian American immigrant, Shirin tells her experiences as a mother raising a child with a dis/ability in the United States.

This is also my story: the story of Kimiya, Shirin's third child and Samin's baby sister. I am an Iranian American education professor and former special education teacher who teaches future educators about the social construction of race and ability, recognizing the limitations of labels of dis/ability, which are constructed by Western cultural norms. I deliberately use the term dis/ability with a slash to problematize and disrupt the negative connotations associated with dis/ability, which are often highly influenced by cultural norms. I value marginalized voices that are often relegated to the sidelines, especially in traditional research in education. As a higher education teacher who advocates to leave behind dichotomies, especially those that result in an *us versus them* division of the "normal" and "dis/abled" body, I write my story to disrupt misconceptions of living with my sister Samin Banoo, an individual with a dis/ability.

STUDENT REFLECTION: As a teacher of students with disabilities, this "us versus them" mentality has been an unfortunate presence in my work. When students with disabilities are excluded from classes and activities with their peers, it affirms the false belief that there is such thing as normal people and that people with disabilities are on the outside. —Teacher/doctoral student

---

I approach research through a subjective DisCrit lens, which emerges out of Annamma, Connor, and Ferri's (2016) research on the intersection of dis/ability and race. *DisCrit* refers to Dis/ability Critical Race Studies, which combines aspects of critical race theory (CRT) and Disability Studies (DS) to engage in a dual analysis of race and ability (Annamma et al., 2016). This lens recognizes the social construction of dis/ability (Davis, 2010) that, instead of blaming dis/ability as the fault or credit of the individual, determines that the discussion of ability is socially created by a society that needs to make space for all forms of ability. The DisCrit lens also recognizes that race is socially constructed, with the critical emphasis that culturally and linguistically diverse individuals who also have a dis/ability face multiple forms of oppression.

The lived experience is not always easy to write about, especially when it involves retelling the hopes and aspirations of a mother regarding her child with a dis/ability. In this chapter, my mother and I worked together as a team to tell our lived experiences. This was an emotional task and conversation to undertake and write about, which we hope can give a glimpse into the lived experiences, realities, and aspirations of an Iranian American mother who wholeheartedly embraces her child who needs significant support and a sister who recognizes the benefits of her sibling relationship despite the continuous longing to communicate with her.

INTRODUCING SAMIN

I want to begin by introducing the qualities and virtues that make my sister beautiful. My sister, Samin Banoo, is a joyful human being who has a great sense of humor. She is a loving soul who is endlessly patient with her nieces and nephews, who are all under the age of 4. She is empathetic to their needs. She cried when she first met her first-born nephew. The joy that Samin shares with those around her not only can be seen in Photo 6.1 but also felt by anyone who comes in contact with her.

My parents' focus has always been on Samin's happiness, comfort, and well-being. Despite her physical challenges and inability to speak, they were able to identify Samin's loves:

Photo 6.1. Samin Banoo at Her Brother's House, Where She Can Hear All Her Nephews and Nieces Playing Together

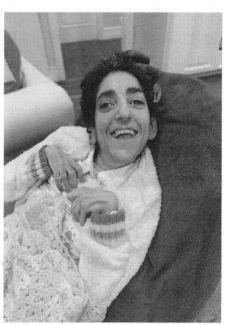

One thing that we know that she always enjoyed: music. My husband made a stack of CDs of prayers, nice music, comforting music, violin, piano, Chopin that we played for her at home. Music is something that was very soothing to her soul and her mind.

Samin enjoyed and benefited from music. Therefore, her teachers and service providers used music as a tool with her.

For preservice and inservice professionals who will work with diverse students with a variety of needs, it is helpful to get to know your students, their personalities, and their backgrounds. Often, collaborating and building rapport with students' families will help you learn about the student, especially in communicating with the student more effectively. In the case of Samin, normative communication did not occur, but reactions like smiling and enjoyment were evident when music was involved. Getting to know the families of students can help professionals gain insights into their students' lives and personalities that can help facilitate learning and growth.

SHIRIN'S STORY

My mother, Shirin, is a woman with deep faith who is dedicated to service to humanity and her family. She is an inclusive woman who is hospitable; her door is always open, and she embodies the Iranian image of being a mother to everyone (Maghzi, 2017). She is an Iranian American woman who is the mother of three. She is a member of the Baháʼí Faith, which is a persecuted religious minority in Iran. Shirin's story begins with her immigration to America:

> My life has been a challenging life, but I am grateful to God for all that He has given me. The mindset I have been given has also been a gift from above; the ability to look at the positives even despite the difficult situations I have experienced in life. I would joyfully accept this life again if God were to give it to me again. I am grateful for all the bounties given to me being a mother of three children, my middle child having been dis/abled due to birth trauma in 1980 when I was in my late twenties.
>
> I immigrated to the United Kingdom in 1972 and then came to the United States in 1974 to further my education, where I met my husband in California at a Baháʼí conference in 1976. That year I married my husband, who had immigrated to the United States in 1970 to attend Oregon State University in Corvallis. The next year, in 1977, I went back to Iran to bring my parents and relocate them to America. Shortly afterward, the Iranian Revolution began; to this day, I have not been back to my motherland due to the persecution that members of my faith face in Iran. As a Baháʼí, we are oppressed people in Iran. If I had raised Samin in Iran, she would have faced double the oppression due to her faith and physical and mental condition.

The immigration experience is one that educators should understand. The move from the home country to America always involves significant changes and may include the loss of both professional and socioeconomic status. Regardless of difficulties with English or apparent socioeconomic status in the United States, the well-informed educator recognizes that parents may have been well educated in their home country.

Discovery and Reaction

Samin's dis/abilities occurred during birthing trauma due to errors in the delivery that resulted in a lack of oxygen for her. This experience shaped the entire family. It changed my parents' lives and the lives of our extended family. It influenced my brother's choice to become a pediatric dentist who specializes in children with dis/abilities and my decision to teach special education and study Dis/ability Studies. My mother recounted learning about Samin's state:

> At the beginning, I was crying a lot. [Emotional] I remember the first time when the pediatric neurologist broke the news to Papa and me. She was not even a year old; she was about six months. She was born in January 1980. Just imagine. They sent us to a pediatric neurologist; then he opened up to us about what happened. He said, exactly, "Your daughter is like an airplane that they put the engine in the back the other way. It's like one switch is off. It has been unplugged. You have to plug it in." We were so perplexed. It was very hard! Her dad lost the ability to speak. That was the first time I saw my husband was crying.

Shirin's and the family's reactions cannot be entirely separated from the cultural context. Dis/ability in Iran is stigmatized and hidden (Goodrich, 2013). However, the Bahá'í writings view dis/ability similarly to differences in any talent or ability, and individuals with disabilities remain equal members within the faith, placing the responsibility on the fellow members of the community to ensure that all individuals can participate and serve (National Spiritual Assembly of the Bahá'ís of the United States, 1998). Family members' reactions fell somewhere between, with an outpouring of grief.

> It was painful for us and it was painful for others, my family members. People—they started coming and visiting us—like, have you ever seen [when] somebody passed away and died? Everybody would come from morning until night, and then at night, when they were leaving, I didn't want anyone to leave. I was afraid of going in [to her] room at night. I was afraid of my own child [crying and very emotional]. I was afraid of her: that beautiful soul that is innocent, that's just a light, and is a pure soul. It was a very, very painful experience, because I guess at that time, I had never ever imagined what a life of a person that is not "normal" [is] like.

This aligns with the research on families' understandings of dis/ability, which has found that social contexts have great influence on parental reactions to dis/ability (Ferguson, 2002). My parents' initial grief and sadness for their daughter was shaped by doctors', friends', and families' reactions to their child. This outpouring of grief and sympathy, paired with cultural Iranian beliefs around hiding dis/ability as shameful (Kashani-Sabet, 2010), informed and shaped their response to their child. This led my mother to fear being alone with her child at night. Unable to express herself, she would cry for hours without end, resulting in monthly visits to the doctor's office and to the hospital. For my mother, this was a vicious cycle. Samin's condition and her abilities were very limiting, and she is still dependent on others' care for survival.

Understanding Motherhood When Raising a Daughter with a Dis/ability

For my mother, raising Samin has become permeated by an overwhelming sense of joy (see Photo 6.2). The stories my mother tells focus on not only the belief that she and her husband were *chosen* to be parents of Samin, but also that she was *called to sacrifice* for her daughter, which aligns with the Bahá'í call for service.

Shirin's story exemplifies the tension for mothers between developing a new understanding of their child, thereby pushing back against the dominant narrative

Photo 6.2. Three Generations of the Family (Shirin, Samin, and Kimiya's Daughter) Smiling in the Kitchen

of dis/ability, or getting stuck in this narrative and hoping for a "normal" child. My mother continued to articulate a new understanding, which she attributed to her faith allowing her to accept Samin:

> I know [that] what is very comforting for me is that—always, I see that Samin, as long as she lives in this world, that it's going to be the world with lots of challenges for her. Maybe she has many [physical] deprivations as far as being in this world, but in the Bahá'í writings, Bahá'u'lláh said [paraphrased]: I understood that the deprived of the world are many, and God has promised to recompense them in the worlds of God. Because this is my personal belief: that this is the womb world for the next [and] she is going to continue her journey through the worlds of God, and that she will be without any dis/abilities and everything will be fine. So a Bahá'í perspective gives you a vision to look at these kinds of issues—like dis/abilities and physical dis/abilities and limitations, mentally or emotionally about someone—to look at it in another light, another shade, that this world is not everything. It's like [we are] traveler[s,] that you just stop, and then, for whatever period of time—like in this place, or in this hotel, or in this house—and then you have to leave and you will continue your journey in the worlds of God. All the physical dis/abilities will go away [as] the next life [is] not a physical world; it's a spiritual world. So what matters is the soul. The Bahá'í writings [talk] about the soul, and the immortality of the soul is important. It is immortal. She hasn't done anything wrong, and she will continue her progress. So this is comforting me, and also comforting me as a mother [who] went through pain and aching inside. [Voice gets emotional]. [Because] I wanted to see how Samin will progress here. I have to accept it and go on. Although it never got easy! You accept it. Accepting is different than getting used to it. It never gets easier for a mother, at least for me. You go on with your life.

Despite her faith and positive outlook on Samin's dis/ability, my mother made clear that she does not wish dis/ability for any mother's child.

> I don't ever wish for any parents or mother to grow spiritually, mentally, and emotionally with such an experience. I hope nobody will go through that route of developing his own character like we went. I never wish anyone to have that, because that is a very painful challenge of life for any mother. It is not easy! I would say it was very difficult. I'm not wishing [this for] any parents. It was a hard life, but it seems that so far, we handled [it]. And don't think it was easy! We practically broke every part of our bodies. I have done that, and her father went through surgery, shoulder surgery. But I love Samin! I love Samin so much! There was not a moment that I didn't want to have her!

While she accepts her daughter's condition, my mother distinguishes this act of acceptance from desiring dis/ability. Nonetheless, my mother believes that she will develop and grow because of this experience with Samin.

My mother is clearly influenced by the *hegemony of normalcy*. Her faith helps her accept Samin, but her acceptance is still based upon the dichotomy of normal/abnormal. Although I want her to resist and push back against it, the early language absorbed from the doctors of *handicapped* is hard for her to overcome. She *does,* however, push back against the Iranian cultural norms of hiding away individuals with dis/abilities.

Despite the difficulties and preparation required to travel with Samin, this did not stop my parents from taking her on family trips around the world when she was a young child. However, as she reached adulthood, it became more and more difficult to travel with her.

> Well, almost whatever activities we had—for example, traveling—we took her to. One trip to Europe, to France, and to Germany, but she was much younger. Then, other trips, [for example] going [to Northern California]. We always took her! But the problem was that Samin gets kind of motion sickness. Like most children in the car, they like to sleep, but for her, she would react differently. By the time we would get to our destination, she was showing much discomfort. But she was always included, and we always took her with us! We took her to Israel, Mount Carmel. That was the highlight of her life and our life with her, because when she got older, it was more difficult to travel that far with her, except going up north. We had to always be careful and get her food ready; everything had to be packed well.

This inclusive approach to supporting a child with dis/abilities may be replicated in the school setting. However, it is important to keep in mind that as my sister grew older, it became more and more difficult to transport her due to her increased weight and spasticity in her limbs. These resulted in complications when attending different functions outside the home. These physical changes and greater limitations may be a reality for many of the families.

THE IMPORTANCE OF INTENTIONALITY

The *intentionality* of language for service providers is important, since it influences the language that parents internalize and use to describe their reality. This means considering the intentions of people when they use words and language that refer to dis/ability or any other word that is used to describe someone. According to Freire and Macedo (2003), language, which is constructed, tends to be owned by those with power or in dominant groups and can be used to transform "objective reality" (p. 356; see also Giroux, 2003). Additionally, "only those who have power can generalize and decree their group characteristics as representative of the national culture" (Freire & Macedo, 2003, p. 357–358). This power over language ultimately leads to determining who has access to resources:

> Constructions of race, sex and gender, sexual orientation, and disability [are] constructed through social processes in which categories of people are (1) named, (2) aggregated and disaggregated, (3) dichotomized and stigmatized, and (4) denied the attributes valued in the culture. (Gordon & Rosenblum, 2001, p. 6)

Service providers, being in a position of power, should consider the *intentionality* behind the terms and language they use with families and children. Service providers should consider how their tone and words influence the way families and their children regard themselves.

For my family, we grew up speaking "Finglisi," a combination of Farsi and English. The words we were given to describe my sister came from the medical professionals and service providers. Terms and phrases such as *vegetable, handicapped,* and *brain-damaged* were used in the household to describe Samin. It was not until I was a student of dis/ability studies that I understood the horror of the language we had been given. Although words such as *cripple, vegetable, dumb, deformed, retard[ed],* and *gimp* have been removed from public conversation, they continue to be used in the discourse of mainstream society despite their negative power and influence. These "nasty words" are understood to be rude and vindictive, yet they continue to be used in jokes, casual narratives, and metaphors (Linton, 1998). Even the metaphoric use of these terms continues to stigmatize individuals with dis/abilities:

> When we use terms like "retarded," "lame," or "blind"— even if we are referring to acts or ideas and not to people at all—we perpetuate the stigma associated with disability. By using a label, which is commonly associated with disabled people to denote deficiency, a lack, or an ill-conceived notion, we reproduce the oppression of people with disabilities. (Ben-Moshe, 2005, p. 107)

The intention and use of these words by my parents were not derogatory; these were simply the only words they had been given by medical professionals to explain Samin's circumstance.

The concept of intentionality and family limitations with language intersect. Family members are often limited by the availability of words to describe their children, especially for immigrant families who are English language learners. Thus it is vital to get to know the child and their family, regardless of what language is used, and to develop a cultural proficiency for understanding the family's perspective and culture. Asking families how they would describe their children, including words they use in their mother tongue, can be helpful to contextualize how families view their child, but only with an understanding of possible effects from cultural context, cultural differences in perceiving dis/ability, and linguistic differences.

DENIAL, DESPERATION, AND RELIGION

As the youngest child, I grew up hearing my mother's story about love and service throughout my life. My sister is my sister, and I love her. However, the positive views of the love and service perspectives developed over time; Samin's diagnosis initially resulted in denial and desperation that were only later tempered by belief.

Denial

Initially, before Samin's official diagnosis, Shirin's family and friends hoped Samin would get better. Over time, the severity became evident. Even though Samin had muscle, leg, and joint issues, her doctor recommended against surgery:

> Her brain condition and her bodily condition was so fragile, and she was so weak. Samin never [was] able to pick up one spoon or one toy, never had the ability to hold anything! Even for 30 seconds in her hands! Then, later on, she had dislocated joints, they said because of spasticity. I took her to [the] orthopedic surgeon, bless his soul, if he is not around. He said, "You don't want to have this child have an operation because she doesn't have pain from her hips. There is no need for her to have the surgery. It's more pain, more agony."

In addition to her orthopedic difficulties, Samin has serious stomach issues and acid reflux.

Desperation and Religion

My parents were so desperate for a solution to Samin's condition that they tried various pseudoscientific programs that claimed they could help. In fact, on a friend's recommendation, they took Samin to see a televangelist who advertised praying over individuals with dis/abilities to cure them.

> Being a Bahá'í, we believe science and religion go hand in hand, but as parents, we were so perplexed, and we were trying, hanging [on]to any hope that possibly will tell us, that maybe, there is a remedy and hope she gets better. They said [the televangelist] has special hands, and she puts her hands on [the individual with a dis/ability to be cured]. And I do believe that some people, they have a special energy that they can give. Maybe because this lady was [a] very devoted Christian, that's how she thought she was helping, but of course, from the beginning, I told my husband, "That is impossible! But if you want to go, let's go!" My husband wanted to go so we took her!

Given my parents' devotion to the Bahá'í faith, this anecdote shows their desperation to help Samin. As Bahá'ís believe in the harmony of science and religion, it would be unusual for a Bahá'í to trust that a self-proclaimed healer could help their child when there is no scientific evidence for that phenomenon.

While the foray into televangelism was less than effective, to this day, my mother has a deep faith in God. Similar to Jegatheesan's (2009) study reporting that immigrant families might also see their child with dis/abilities as a blessing, influenced by her Bahá'í Faith and its emphasis on service to humanity, my mother believes that Samin is providing her and my father with the opportunity to be of service:

> It's just in this life she [is] with me and is giving me the opportunity for service. Maybe I was not, or I wouldn't have the ability, or I wouldn't give service like that to anybody—only my own loved ones—so she came to my life. And I have been, and my husband—we are the chosen ones for Samin, to deal with her every day. I always thought that whatever we have is a gift and blessing of the High Above. I look at Samin as a gift from God, because she gave me and her father an opportunity to be of service. Service to my own daughter, to my own child. We all can serve at different capacities.

Thus Shirin's beliefs as a Bahá'í help her recognize the meaning in Samin's life and her purpose in the world.

Despite Samin's limitations, my mother views my sister as a silent teacher who has helped her spread the Bahá'í Faith's message of love and unity. Shirin expressed that it is of the utmost importance to her, since "Nothing is compare[d] to th[is]!" This strengthens her belief that her daughter is a blessing, while at the same time, it aids in supporting her faith in God. Although public schools believe in the separation between church and state, it is important for teachers and service professionals to learn how culture and religion affect views of dis/ability and how parents approach life with their child (Maghzi, 2017).

BARRIERS TO HOME–SCHOOL COLLABORATION

It is difficult for my mother to critique her interactions with Samin's school, teachers, and service providers, since deference and respect to professionals is integrated into our culture's behavioral expectations. While this makes it challenging for her to comment on the barriers of home–school collaboration with service providers, she eventually admitted to problems with blame, navigating the IEP process, and negligence.

STUDENT REFLECTION: It is easy in a teacher prep program to say, "I'm going to be aware of the cultural deference to professionals when I'm in the field." However, awareness is simply not enough. The onus is on school professionals to ensure that families have the most comprehensive information about their child's education programming while proactively taking steps to empower families to question us so-called experts. —Graduate student

---

Parental Blame

Most Iranian American families adhere to a medicalized approach to dis/ability (Tarian, 2014), creating a dichotomy of normal/abnormal. In the Iranian culture there is a desire for perfection and success (Tarian, 2014), making it difficult for families to initially embrace their children's differences. Especially in Iran, these attitudes result in individuals with dis/abilities experiencing stigma (Dehnavi, Malekpour, Faramarzi, & Talebi, 2011; Tarian, 2014), blame being placed upon their mothers (Jalali-Kushki, 2015), and families hiding their child's dis/ability (McConkey & Samadi, 2013).

For my mother, despite her complete devotion to Samin, she felt blamed by service providers in America for Samin's lack of progress while in therapy. Although these service providers claimed they could remedy Samin's situation, they failed to help alleviate Shirin's unease, and instead contributed to feelings of guilt and blame. She recounted one instance in which Samin attended a program that claimed to help individuals with dis/abilities, but made little to no progress:

> "I feel that every time I was going there," I told my husband, I said, "I'm going to a trial." Like I'm going to the court, and in front of the judge and jury, and they are questioning me, and they are giving me the guilt feeling that I did not do a good job.

This sense of being blamed was complicated by Iranian cultural norms. The stigma of dis/ability is so entrenched in Iranian culture that Iranian American mothers feared disclosing their children's diagnoses (Tarian, 2014), and often feared reaching out to connect with other families and parents with children with dis/abilities (McConkey & Samadi, 2013). Due to the stigma regarding dis/ability, although Iran is considered to be a collectivist society (Tarian, 2014), Iranians are less likely to access social support when raising a child with a dis/ability (Davis, 2010; McConkey & Samadi, 2013). The stigma in Iranian culture regarding dis/ability has resulted in families shying away from one another and not reaching out to one another for mutual support and assistance.

Each culture will have different views and reactions to individuals with dis/abilities and their families. In Iran, individuals with dis/abilities are often hidden and their family members as a result are isolated (Artounian, Shariati, Amini, Salimi, & Nejatisafa, 2012; Goodrich, 2014; Tarian, 2014) and hesitant to reach out to connect with other families and parents with children with dis/abilities (McConkey & Samadi, 2013). When families of individuals with dis/abilities continuously deal with a sense of judgment from others (Jalali-Kushki, 2015; Tarian, 2014), it is important for school professionals and service providers to respect the decisions that mothers and families make regarding their child.

Despite the severe stigma regarding dis/ability in their culture, my parents pushed back against public attitudes and suggestions to abandon my sister.

I knew this [Iranian American] lady and she was getting her doctorate degree from UCLA. And with all her knowledge and everything, she came right to us and very frank[ly] and . . . blunt[ly] said, "I don't understand why should you have this child and keep her at home when you know that she is not going to be anything!" She was in a little bassinet in the corner of the room not doing any harm to anybody! [My husband,] [who] is a very gentle soul [who] never ever dislikes anyone or say anything negative about anybody, turned to me and said, "Oh my God, your friend is a monster! She is not a human being with a human heart! How could someone come to somebody and [say] just put her away because she cannot be like other children," because then what is our duty as parents and mother and father who brought a child to this world? I tell you, even close family members had the same [mentality].

Despite being confronted by attitudes in public spaces that suggested they should hide Samin, my parents made it a priority to have Samin included in all of our family gatherings and faith-based events whenever possible (see Photo 6.3).

Photo 6.3. A Photo of the Family on Kimiya and Shawn's Wedding Day on September 28, 2007

Pictured left to right: Samin's brother, Amir Sanah; her father, Sam; Samin; her sister, Kimiya; her mother, Shirin Banoo; and her new brother, Shawn

Experiences with the IEP Process

My mother acknowledged that if they were less proficient in the English language, she and my father would have experienced significantly more stress and difficulty navigating the special education system. My mother recounted many papers (in English) given to them with an expectation to read. Shirin mentioned that she had very little time to read these documents since she was raising three children with various needs, but she was grateful my father was able to read and make sense of them.

> A systematic communication was lacking to inform us about the services that were available to us. We had to try to familiarize ourselves with the resources and papers which were given to us. However, my reality was that I had two other children and had limited time to read through all the papers, which were given to us. I am lucky my husband was able to put in the time and read these papers and documents on behalf of us.

Shirin expressed her concern for parents who would not be able to read all the forms and papers, although she did acknowledge that interpreters were provided to parents who did not fluently speak English at the IEP meetings.

> We were always included in the IEP process. They always called us and let us know about the meetings. To some extent, they were very unrealistic about their goals for my daughter. For example, they said she was going to grab and hold an object for one minute. To this day, she is 39 years old and she has not done this! Or that Samin was going to sit up without any support and control her body. These are called unrealistic goals! Maybe their goal was to give us hope, which was very nice. However, this could result in false hope for parents who saw the educators as specialist and did not question their ideas.
>
> Although they asked for parent input at the meeting, they never consulted with us regarding IEP goals prior to our meeting. Sincerity and realistic goals would be helpful for students at their perceived level of functioning. Creating an atmosphere for students to achieve their goals is important but in the case of my daughter, these goals were never met. Deep down it really didn't feel that great that these goals they set were not met. This led me to not wanting to participate a few times over the years in the IEP process. This was frustrating and disappointing; of course, we came to accept this reality.
>
> My husband and I were more concerned about the comfort of our daughter. We wanted Samin to not suffer from pain and be comfortable, enjoy her schooling. More attention could have been placed in finding supports to help make this happen. From finding her a wheelchair that would help mold to her body that wouldn't result in sores. It's important to ask questions and clarify the words that are used in these meetings.

STUDENT REFLECTION: The value that Shirin and her husband place on comfort and well-being for Samin is an important message for teachers. With
our focus on our curriculum and all of our other obligations, teachers can
lose sight of what will support each individual with a disability to have a life
of quality. Parents care deeply for the happiness of their children throughout
their life, and it is so valuable when parents remind us of how important this
is. —Teacher/doctoral student

My mother noted that her language abilities helped her navigate the system;
this led her to coach other families and parents. The principal at Samin's school
asked Shirin to become a mentor who welcomed bilingual parents and help them
transition their child with a dis/ability into the school.

> We had a loving and kind principal for our daughter. She asked me to take
> on a service role and welcome the new parents to our school and help them
> as their child transitioned to the school and programs. We were particularly
> grateful to [the principal] as she informed us about services that we were
> entirely unaware of! For example, we were purchasing our diapers with our
> own money! Until the principal informed us that our daughter qualified for
> free diapers.

Shirin took pride in providing this type of service to parents and helping them
as they became familiar with the school. She also acknowledged that a language
barrier existed, contributing to the difficulty navigating the IEP process and special education system for many of these parents.

Negligence

Shirin wanted to focus on the positives in her relationship with her daughter's
teachers and school professionals, and yet she could not avoid recognizing that
barriers to communication with these professionals did exist.

> These barriers to communication paired with negligent actions continue to
> affect the life of my daughter to this day. In the case of one emergency, where
> our daughter Samin was affected by teacher negligence, our child should
> have been taken to the hospital.

At school, an aide who assisted with Samin fell on her, resulting in her feeding
tube being pulled out of her stomach. The school waited to get in contact with
my mother and father instead of calling emergency services. The school's lack of
urgency resulted in Samin's feeding tube hole closing up.

This negligence was also evident in her adult home care facility. From my
mother's perspective, this lifelong obligation of tending to their child continues

even though Samin no longer resides at home. According to my mother, the home care facility provides Samin with only minimal care lacking in attention to detail for Samin's personal hygiene. Since Samin is not able to advocate for herself, my mother takes on advocacy for her daughter as her own responsibility. Due to the home care facility not providing adequate care, Shirin feels the need to regularly fill in the gaps in her daughter's care. In addition to cooking for Samin, my mother also assists in showering my sister and grooming her. Furthermore, my mother works hard to hydrate Samin, because although the home gives Samin a large amount of fiber, they do not provide her with a sufficient amount of water, thereby causing her to become so constipated that even suppositories do not work. My mother feels that it is her responsibility as a mother to provide the care that the facility overlooks. She also mentions that her husband helps with Samin's grooming. He has driven 3 hours to come give her a bath. Thus, while Samin's visits require large amounts of my mother's time and energy, she is not alone in the work.

TEAM PARENTING

In Iranian culture mothers are the primary caregivers of their children (Alizadeh & Andries, 2002). As a result, Iranian mothers of children with dis/abilities often find themselves committing themselves to their children mentally, emotionally, and physically (Kermanshahi, Vanaki, Ahmadi, Kazemnejad, & Azadfalah, 2008). In Bahá'í literature, women have an important role as the primary educators of the future generation ('Abdu'l-Bahá, 1909/1916). According to Bahá'í writings, women and men are equal in the sight of God, and true progress for humanity is impossible unless and until both men and women work together for society to progress (Bahá'u'lláh, 'Abdu'l-Bahá, Shoghi Effendi, & Universal House of Justice, 1986).

My parents often worked together to help each other support Samin because of the realities of raising a child with a dis/ability. Their cooperation was not tied overtly to cultural or religious beliefs, but it still exemplified the Bahá'í call for equality. Shirin was very emotional as she recalled that at night, my parents took shifts "taking care of [Samin]. So he never left me alone in that journey. Most of the time she was in our bed. I remember how it was very hard." Much of my mother's story recalled my father team-parenting with her:

> At my age now, I kind of sit back and watch what the rest of my life will be with her, because I might not be around and she might still be living! My experience is I would tell anyone who has this kind of children to accept it and go on with your life. Don't try to change anything. If you can help the situation, you can make the person put her or him in comfort, you do that. That is what I have done as an experienced mother. In that journey, I can say my husband was involved and dedicated to that. Because this is not only two hands of mothers who are taking care of the child but rather accompaniment is something that is always needed any time you have a goal and want to

reach that. With my child, Samin, accompaniment of her dad was very important.

Sharing the journey of rearing Samin with her husband differed from the literature about Iranian mothers rearing their children (Kermanshahi et al., 2008). Therefore, it is important for teachers and service providers to get to know their students and their families and learn about their expectations for rearing a child with unique abilities and limitations.

Among the difficulties of raising a daughter with dis/abilities, my parents often got little to no sleep. However, they worked together to make sure to not complain and to keep the atmosphere as routine as possible.

So it was difficult, but between my husband and I, we managed it well, but we never opened up to anybody about pain. Our home was the home of love and laughter. As much as at night we wouldn't sleep, as much as Samin had all this pain, but all the kids—children in the family—they would come there [to] play. We tried to keep everything as healthy, and as "normal," as possible because we didn't want people not to come because we constantly complain about our pain and what we go through.

This need for normalcy demonstrates the impact of the hegemony of normalcy on Shirin's daily language and perspective. However, my parents also pushed back against Iranian culture of hiding individuals with dis/abilities.

For [my husband] and I that was a pain because we wanted, we were taking her everywhere. . . . We didn't have any hidden agenda. We said, "This is it. This is our daughter! We are not going to come if we cannot bring her!" Any celebration or anything going on in our families' or relatives' house, my brother-in-law, we always take Samin and they are always with open arms to her and they love her.

Despite the family's inclusion of Samin, extended family still sometimes questioned my parents' physical health as Samin grew older and heavier, resulting in disapproval for lifting her or bringing her to family gatherings.

At the same time, even though they love her, they are thinking honestly about me and [my husband] too, your dad. "Enough is enough, you have done everything! Why are you, you have just invested your health in your child. How much more do you want to do?"

Caring for their daughter at home for 26 years greatly impacted the physical health of Shirin and her husband, resulting in several surgeries for both parents. Consequently, they were encouraged by their two other children to place their daughter into a home care facility. Even after placing her there, and despite their own bodily ailments and limitations, they continue to bring Samin to their family home on weekends in order to care for her themselves. Shirin expressed that caring for her child is a lifelong commitment:

> We have been nonstop involved with Samin, and I think until the ends of our lives, as long as we live, we will be involved—unless she dies before us. You know, even now that we have placed her in a home—because for 26 years, faithfully we took care of her at home, and if my husband's shoulder wouldn't go for operation, and if my back and my knees wouldn't be affected like that, probably still she would have been at home.

Even after undergoing bilateral knee and spinal surgeries, my mother continues to bring my sister home regularly to tend to her—a job that requires significant mental, emotional, and physical exertion. "I try to cook for her, feed her . . . clean her . . . do the little things that, for me, it's kind of like I'm doing as a mother. I am contributing to her well-being."

FINAL THOUGHTS FROM SHIRIN

Overall, my mother spoke passionately about her lived experiences raising Samin. At times, it was emotionally trying to listen to her stories due to my deeply personal connection as Shirin's daughter and Samin's sister. For my mother, her lived experience emerges out of a story about self-sacrifice and being "chosen." On the other hand, my mother viewed this as an opportunity and a bounty given to our family in order for them to grow. She recounts the positive impact Samin has had on her relationship with my father, as well as the effect of Samin's dis/ability on her other children and extended family:

> Instead of looking at Samin as a misery of my life, I always look at her as an opportunity and bounty that has been given to my family. In many ways, she was the—like a source of bringing my husband and I closer together, also helping my other two children learn more about appreciating who they are and also what has been given to them as far as health. And also, she has a positive impact on the life of other cousins that were around. You know, directly and indirectly. They have more sympathy toward people that are less fortunate as far as health and ability.

According to my mother, Shirin, caring for an individual with a dis/ability has various requirements, love being one of the most necessary. However, the other elements are also essential, including facilities, equipment, and professional help and care to meet her physical needs.

Shirin shared that the act of mothering Samin has never stopped and will continue until the end of Shirin's life. My mother expressed that she has always done whatever is in her capacity to help Samin make progress:

> I have done whatever was in my ability and energy that I had to invest, to push Samin, my daughter, for the little bit of progress, and I never stopped that. So my parenting toward Samin has never stopped. When you have a child with special needs, as long as you live, if truly you want to fulfill your responsibility as a mother, it will continue till the time that you are not in this world.

In the end, Shirin stated that she and her husband take life one day at a time:

> Honestly, you go day by day now! You just go day by day. Actually, all these years, we probably went day by day. It was lots of hope and lots of expectations. You really came down to the reality and accepted the reality.

CONCLUSION

Understanding that each family and culture views dis/ability differently is an important idea to grasp. Families are undoubtedly affected by dominant culture and narrative of dis/ability despite religious ideals and teachings. Therefore, it is important for practitioners to investigate the influence of faith and culture on family belief systems about dis/ability and views of their child. A greater understanding of the intersection of how culture and faith influence parent perspectives on dis/ability contributes to more effective communication and services among service providers, teachers, students, and families to meet student needs (Jegatheesan, Miller, & Fowler, 2010; Lo, 2012). This includes checking for communication clarity (Lo, 2012), understanding of cultural and religious differences that affect parental attitudes, respecting the home culture, and recognizing how religious background in addition to culture and language affect parents' understanding of dis/ability, their child, and the educator (Chun & Fisher, 2014) so we can work together to promote student success in schools.

NOTE

1. Kimiya Maghzi, author of Chapter 6, would like to thank her mother and sister, who have both fueled her passions in life. The chapter was written with them "in her heart, and without them both this chapter would not be possible to write." Kimiya adds, "Special thanks to Mommy Joon for always being an example of persistence, selflessness, love, and strength. You have taught me so much, and I am forever grateful to you. Your devoted mothering to my sister, Samin, has been the driving force behind what I write about and

---

REFLECTION QUESTIONS

- How does the hegemony of normalcy influence Shirin's perspective and language about her daughter? How does the hegemony of normalcy influence your language? How does it influence the language used in schools and in our society?
- Why is intentionality important when considering language? How can we create awareness about the use of certain words and their impact? How is intentionality important across all areas of difference: dis/ability, race, class, gender, sexual orientation, religion, ethnicity, culture, and age?
- The concepts of blame and stigma run through both the literature mentioned and the stories from Shirin and Kimiya. Where have you seen blame and/or stigma associated with dis/ability emerge within education? Can blame and/or stigma associated with dis/ability be found in other cultures? Explain.
- When telling her story, Kimiya always names disability as dis/ability. Why do you think she does this? How does it change your vision and/or thinking about ability?
- Shirin critiqued the IEP process. How would you use Shirin's experience to avoid the pitfalls she describes? How do you assure that goals are within a child's reach? How can paperwork, language, and accessibility be taken into account during IEP meetings? How could you make the IEP experience easier and more accessible for the culturally or linguistically diverse parent(s)?

---

engage in as a scholar. I would like to thank my sister, Samin, who has always been my source of inspiration. You are an angel on Earth who has helped me love more deeply, strive to be better, and work toward advocating for individuals with dis/abilities and their families. My children are so lucky to have you as their Khaleh Samin. I would also like to thank my friend Marni, who is always encouraging me to dedicate time to writing my story. Thank you for your support and encouragement."

REFERENCES

'Abdu'l-Bahá. (1909). *Tablets of Abdul-Baha Abbas*. Chicago, IL: Bahai Publishing Society.

Alizadeh, H., & Andries, C. (2002). Interaction of parenting styles and attention deficit hyperactivity disorder in Iranian parents. *Child & Family Behavior Therapy, 24*(3), 37–52. doi:10.1300/J019v24n03_03

Annamma, S. A., Connor, D. J., & Ferri, B. A. (2016). Dis/ability critical race studies (DisCrit): Theorizing at the intersections of race and dis/ability. In D. J. Connor, B. A. Ferri,

& S. A. Annamma (Eds.), *DisCrit disability studies and critical race theory in education* (pp. 9–32). New York, NY: Teachers College Press.

Artounian, V., Shariati, B., Amini, H., Salimi, A., & Nejatisafa, A. (2012). Persian translation of perception of psychiatry survey questionnaire and evaluation of its psychometric properties. *Iranian Journal of Psychiatry, 7*(3), 135–139. Available at www.ncbi.nlm.nih.gov/pmc/articles/PMC3488869/pdf/IJPS-7-135.pdf

Bahá'u'lláh, 'Abdu'l-Bahá, Shoghi Effendi, & Universal House of Justice. (1986). *Women: Extracts from the writings of Bahá'u'lláh, 'Abdu'l-Bahá, Shoghi Effendi, and the Universal House of Justice.* Wilmette, IL: Bahá'í Publishing Trust.

Ben-Moshe, L. (2005). "Lame idea": Disabling language in the classroom. In L. Ben-Moshe, R. C. Cory, M. Feldbaum, & K. Sagendorf (Eds.), *Building pedagogical curb cuts: Incorporating disability in the university classroom and curriculum* (pp. 107–116). Syracuse, NY: Syracuse University.

Chun, M., & Fisher, M. E. (2014). Crossroads: The intersection of affirming cultural and neurological diversity. *NYS TESOL Journal, 1*(2), 105–121.

Davis, L. J. (2010). Constructing normalcy. In L. Davis (Ed.), *The disability studies reader* (pp. 4–19). New York, NY: Routledge.

Dehnavi, S. R., Malekpour, M., Faramarzi, S., & Talebi, H. (2011). The share of internalized stigma and autism quotient in predicting the mental health of mothers with autism children in Iran. *International Journal of Business and Social Science, 2*(20), 251–259.

Ferguson, P. M. (2002). Mapping the family: Disability studies and the exploration of parental response to disability. In G. L. Albrecht, K. Seelman, & M. Bury (Eds.), *Handbook of disabiltiy studies* (pp. 373– 395). Thousand Oaks, CA: Sage.

Freire, P., & Macedo, D. (2003). Rethinking literacy: A diologue. In A. Darder, M. Baltodano, & R. D. Torres (Eds.), *The critical pedagogy reader* (pp. 354–364). New York, NY: RoutledgeFalmer.

Giroux, H. A. (2003). Critical theory and educational practice. In A. Darder, M. Baltodana, & R. D. Tores (Eds.), *The critical pedagogy reader* (pp. 27–56). New York, NY: RoutledgeFalmer.

Goodrich, N. H. (2013). Lifetime struggle: A family narration of disability experience in Iran. *Review of Disability Studies: An International Journal, 9*(2/3), 54–62.

Goodrich, N. H. (2014). A Persian Alice in disability literature wonderland: Disability studies in Iran. *Disability Studies Quarterly, 34*(2), 9. Retrieved from doi:http://dx.doi.org/10.18061/dsq.v34i2.4255

Gordon, B. O., & Rosenblum, K. E. (2001). Bringing disability into the sociological frame: A comparison of disability with race, sex, and sexual orientation statuses. *Disability & Society, 16*(1), 5–19. doi:10.1080/09687590020020831

Jalali-Kushki, Y. (2015). A narrative inquiry: Experiences of Iranian mothers of children with disabilities in Toronto, Ontario (Unpublished doctoral dissertation). McGill University, Montreal, Canada.

Jegatheesan, B. (2009). Cross-cultural issues in parent–professional interactions: A qualitative study of perceptions of Asian American mothers of children with developmental disabilities. *Research & Practice for Persons with Severe Disabilities, 34*(3/4), 123–136. doi:10.2511/rpsd.34.3-4.123

Jegatheesan, B., Miller, P. J., & Fowler, S. A. (2010). Autism from a religious perspective: A study of parental beliefs in South Asian Muslim immigrant families. *Focus on Autism and Other Developmental Disabilities, 25*(2), 98–109. doi:10.1177/1088357610361344

Kashani-Sabet, F. (2010). The haves and the have nots: A historical study of disability in modern Iran. *Iranian Studies, 43*(2), 167–195. Retrieved from www.tandfonline.com/doi/abs/10.1080/00210860903541947 doi:10.1080/00210860903541947

Kermanshahi, S., Vanaki, Z., Ahmadi, F., Kazemnejad, A., & Azadfalah, P. (2008). Children with learning disabilities: A phenomenological study of the lived experiences of Iranian mothers. *International Journal of Qualitative Studies on Health and Well-Being, 3*(1), 18–26. Retrieved from www.tandfonline.com/doi/full/10.1080/17482620701757284

Linton, S. (1998). *Claiming disability: Knowledge and identity.* New York, NY: NYU Press.

Lo, L. (2012). Demystifying the IEP process for diverse parents of children with disabilities. *Teaching Exceptional Children, 44*(3), 14–20.

Maghzi, K. S. (2017). *The dance of motherhood: Exploring the lived experiences of Iranian-American mothers raising individuals with dis/abilities* (Unpublished doctoral dissertation). Chapman University, Orange, CA.

McConkey, R., & Samadi, S. A. (2013). The impact of mutual support on Iranian parents of children with an autism spectrum disorder: A longitudinal study. *Disability & Rehabilitation, 35*(9), 775–784. doi:10.3109/09638288.2012.707744

National Spiritual Assembly of the Bahá'ís of the United States. (1998). *Developing distinctive Bahá'í communities: Guidelines for spiritual assemblies.* Wilmette, IL: Bahá'í Publishing Trust.

Tarian, T. (2014). *Experiences of Iranian American mothers with children with autism* (Doctoral dissertation). ProQuest Dissertations & Theses Global database. (1620163001)

CHAPTER 7

A Goat Among Lions

Unveiling the Challenges Faced by a Somali
Refugee Mother of a Child with Autism

Sahra Bashir[1] and Amy Gooden

The Somali of the United States are a diaspora people who fled their native Somalia when their country collapsed in 1991. At that time nearly 1 million Somalis fled Somalia and went to refugee camps in Kenya, Ethiopia, and Djibouti. Affluent Somalis escaped to western Europe and eventually came to the United States. Poverty and civil war have wreaked havoc on the nation of Somalia. The collapse of the Siad Barre regime in early 1991 led to a violent interclan civil war. Since then, more than half the Somali population has been displaced.

Among the thousands of Somali refugees, Somali women and Bantu are particularly disadvantaged groups, since they have low literacy and few transferable skills. Somali refugees are primarily women and children, since many of the men have been killed or are missing (A. Yusuf, personal communication, March 30, 2007). The Somali Bantu are a Niger-Congo-origin ethnic minority refugee group who have suffered years of oppression in Somalia. "They have long been considered second-class citizens in Somali society—exploited as laborers and excluded from education, land ownership, political opportunities and representation" (UNHCR, 2003, para 8). Since the inception of the civil war, persecution and discrimination against them has continued by Somali clan leaders, which has made repatriation impossible. When approached by UNHCR in 1999, the U.S. government agreed to resettle this group. There have been nearly 15,000 Somali Bantu resettled. "Since then, the International Organization for Migration (IOM) has taken over all logistical aspects of the resettlement operation with support from UNHCR" (UNHCR, 2003). The Trump administration's 2017 ban on travel for people from numerous Muslim countries to the United States halted resettlement dreams for thousands of Somali refugees seeking asylum and sheds light on the many nativist myths and misconceptions that exist about members of the Somali diaspora (Hawley, 2019; Niayesh, 2019). Although the UNHCR still continues to resettle Somali refugees in other receiving countries, the United States has since significantly reduced the number of refugees it accepts into the country. Those Somali refugees who have entered the United States often face both racial and religious discrimination.

Somalia is located in the Somali Peninsula, known as the Horn of Africa. Somali culture is deeply rooted in collectivistic tendencies that can be seen in core orientations such as hierarchical power structures, gender norms and divisions, and extended family orientations (Abdullahi, 2001; Hofstede, 2011; Lewis, 2008; Lustig & Koehster, 2017). Abdullahi (2001) notes that Somalia is a patriarchal society with male-dominated power structures in family, social, and political spheres. In traditional Somali culture, men and women have different roles in the society, and some of the gender roles are based on Islam (Harris, 2004). In addition, power is hierarchically structured, and reverence and respectful behavior for authority is a cultural norm. According to Hesse (2010), clans are considered an extended network of family and these communal bonds provide social insurance. Somali culture is interdependent, and the individual's well-being is dependent on the community's well-being (Lewis, 2008; Abdullahi, 2001). The Somali nation is geographically and officially one country, but the people who reside within its borders are divided into distinct and often competing clans and subclans (Hesse, 2010; Lewis, 2008; Starck, 2016).

Islam plays a pivotal role in Somali culture. Typically, Somali Muslim perception is more extended in nature than the Western nuclear view of the family (Alitolppa-Niitamo & Abdullahi, 2002; Harris, 2004). The Somali extended family orientation consists of parents and children, grandparents, uncles and aunts, cousins, and friends (Harris, 2004; Lewis, 2008; Starck, 2016). Parental respect is highly valued in Somali culture, and elderly people are greatly honored (Abdullahi, 2001). As a sign of respect, Somalis living in the United States often send remittances to their friends and relatives in Somalia (Boyle & Ali, 2010).

While Somalis who were born in or who have emigrated to Western cultures at a young age often balance traditional Somali cultural norms with Western norms, making them multicultural in many ways (Alitolppa-Niitamo, 2001), Somalis who come to the United States at an older age tend to maintain Somalia's traditional culture. The characteristics of the collectivistic Somali family model and hierarchical social structures are very different from the Western egalitarian and individualistic family models and social structures. Sometimes this can create intergenerational tensions or misunderstandings within families during the acculturation process (Alitolppa-Niitamo, 2010).

Somali culture is recognized worldwide for its rich historic and contemporary art traditions, such as music, art, pottery, and architecture. The renowned poetry of Somalis who live in the Horn of Africa, as well as the Somali diaspora, has brought them international recognition. Sir Richard Burton, an English traveler and a scholar in the field of Arabic studies who visited Somalia in 1854, reported: "The country teems with poets" (Kapchits, 1998, p. 217). Somali oral traditions include an appreciation for alliterative poetry and narrative storytelling. The best poems and verses of outstanding Somali poets have been thoroughly recorded and, in many cases, translated for international audiences. An insufficient number of their proverbs and folktales have been published in Somali (which only became a written language in 1973) or have been translated into European languages (Kapchits, 1998). One major functional obstacle for many Somali refugees emigrating to Western cultures is adjusting from a society that places emphasis primarily on oral literacy to one that relies heavily on print literacy. In this chapter we learn about some of the talents of a Somali family who emigrated to the United States. See Photo 7.1 for one of the many celebrated drawings created by high school student Qalid (a pseudonym). Qalid was diagnosed with autism, and his mother, Sahra (also a pseudonym), is our storyteller here.

People with disabilities living in Somali society experience shame, stigma, and exclusion (Cavallera et al., 2016; Starck, 2016). According to Hasnain, Cohon Shaikh, and Shanawani (2008), disability is not widely discussed even among Somali diaspora communities, and full inclusion has not yet been achieved. In traditional Somali culture, disability is generally associated with physical impairments only, and intellectual disabilities are considered taboo (Rohwerder, 2018). Comprehensive information on the number and situations of people with disabilities in Somalia is lacking. However, most estimates suggest that the percentage is likely to be higher than the global estimate of 15% because of the long period of conflict, poverty, and lack of access to health care (Sida, 2014).

Photo 7.1. Qalid's Abstract Pencil Drawing

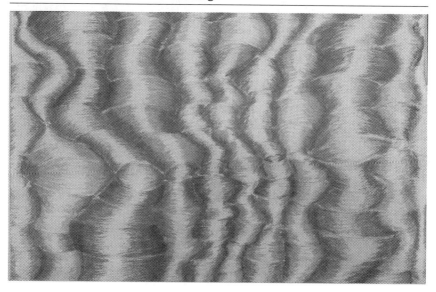

GACMO IS DHAAFAA GACALO KA TIMAADDAA:
LOVE EMERGES WHEN HANDS GIVE SOMETHING TO EACH OTHER.

On a sunny spring day in Boston, there was a room full of about fifteen Somali women at a local conference, which focused on supporting bilingual families of children with disabilities. Four of the women were Somali Bantu and one was a young, teenage Somali student, who expressed that she lamented the loss of oral tradition in her family and explained her desire to author a book of Somali stories. Also in the room were the two female facilitators (Janet and Amy), faculty from a nearby university who had prepared a PowerPoint series on topics such as "How to successfully engage in the IEP process" and "Cross-cultural comparison between U.S. and Somali cultures and expectations of schools." The men had just left upon my (Amy's) arrival, probably due to Somali cultural gender norms, in which mothers are the ones generally responsible for ensuring the educational outcomes of children in Somali families. As we presented various slides, our conversations and exchanges of ideas wandered off topic, but the authentic, informal sharing of personal stories allowed for deeper connections to emerge among the women.

As the session concluded, the women moved about, and I noticed one of the women, Sahra, gifting my colleague and co-presenter (Janet) her own headscarf. As we were all women in the room, Sahra permitted herself to remove her vibrantly patterned headscarf, and meticulously wrap it around Janet's face. Looking a little touched and a little perplexed, Janet tried to politely refuse, but Sahra kindly and firmly insisted that she accept this gesture of friendship. Sahra assured her that she had another scarf in her bag that she could wear upon leaving the room. I also noticed that Janet, in turn, brought baked pastries from a New England pastry shop to our follow-up meeting. Although these exchanges may seem trivial, they helped to break down barriers typical of researcher versus participant, and allowed for a friendly, comfortable, and even loving atmosphere. Due to the importance placed on relationship building in collectivistic cultural contexts, such as the Somali context, this humanistic atmosphere allowed for Sahra's story to emerge authentically.

I was invited to co-present at the conference, and later into the book project, as a cultural broker. I had experience with the Somali community and understanding of their common expectations of students' and teachers' roles in learning. I understood tensions between the American individualistic and the Somali collectivistic classrooms. During our initial conversations, Sahra and I passionately exchanged stories about misunderstandings, myths, and misconceptions that prevail about the Somali diaspora in the United States. Sahra told me that she has been accepted into a master's program in public health, where she plans to pursue a degree that will enable her to "open the eyes" of health professionals working with Somali families. She asked me if I knew of any programs that would help her develop her academic writing in English. I was teaching the Writing Workshop for international, nonnative-English-speaking students at my university and invited her to audit some of the course sessions. These weekly classes provided us with the opportunity to develop our own relationship, and build upon the interview data Janet already had collected from Sahra's visit to her class as a guest speaker.

During an informal interview between Sahra, Janet, and me, Sahra said her "robot" days of taking the kids to and from school, working, and taking care of the household were winding down. She wanted to focus on herself for the first time since leaving Somalia and return to her own education. She also wanted to help others, other "less fortunate Somali families" of children with disabilities. Sahra's interest in sharing her story in this book is based in her belief that knowledge is power. Just as she hopes her work with health professionals can improve the communication with and services for Somali families, Sahra hopes education professionals will learn from her story more effective ways to engage CLD families in schools, especially in the special education process.

Due to the highly sensitive nature of her refugee story and the interclan rivalry that still exists within the Somali diaspora, Sahra asked that we provide a pseudonym. She entrusted us to use this data to coauthor her story. I consider her a coauthor, even though for her own protection, she prefers not to be recognized. We do not value oracy in academia as a form of literacy; however, traditions, knowledge, and wisdom are passed down through stories in Somali culture. Indigenous ways of knowing and communicating information are equally as viable and in some ways more impactful then traditional Western ways of organizing information.

When I met with Sahra both in my Writing Workshop course and alone over coffee (when not formally interviewing), she would often speak to me using the unique rhetorical conventions of Somali oral tradition, beginning each conversation with proverbial lessons. In an effort to capture and honor this tradition, in which stories are told and anchored around proverbs that teach a moral, this chapter is organized thematically by proverb, not traditional Western subheadings.

KHAYR WAX KUUMA DHIMEE SHAR U TOG HAY: IN GOOD TIMES, BE READY FOR BAD TIMES (BECAUSE TIMES ALWAYS CHANGE).

Sahra is a mother of five boys; she came to Boston as a refugee from Somalia during the civil war in the year 1993, after living for a number of years in a refugee camp in Kenya. A significant Somali refugee population made its way to Kenya and has been residing there in camps for the past 2 decades. Sahra's brother sponsored her and her family after she spent 2 years and 8 months in the refugee camp. As a member of the upper class, Sahra explains, she lived quite well in Somalia and had the means and social capital to flee the country as soon as the war broke out. She was 19 at the time and came with her parents and her 3-year-old son and has been living in Boston since then. Her husband, a businessman, was in Italy at the time of her escape and they were separated for a length of time. She had a hard time sponsoring him but finally reunited with him after a total of 5 years.

When asked about how she would like us to refer her background in this book, she passionately explains:

> I am a Somali refugee. The difference between an immigrant and refugee is that I would not have come here if the civil war did not break out in my country. I was living quite well in fact. I understand how health care professionals and school administrators may perceive me here, as a minority, and the games they play or lack of understanding they may have for people who look or dress like me; these are the same games my own people played on the minority (Bantu) population in my country. Back in Somalia, we had a beautiful home; I lived much better than how we live here. I had a private driver to take me places. My brother was studying in the United States. Luckily, because of our resources, we were able to be one of the first groups to escape the country. I had the means that others in my country do not have.

In an excerpt from one of Sahra's class presentations, she described her escape from war-torn Somalia:

> When the civil war happened, my husband was on business in Italy so we got separated. So I came here with my parents, and my husband joined [me] 2 years later . . . because he didn't have a paper to come. That's what happened. I came here as a refugee in 1993, from Somalia, and I came with my family and my son who was almost 3 years old when we came here. My oldest son. And my brother was here prior to the civil war to go to law school. So because of him, he sponsored us from the refugee camp, and that is how we came here. If you have a family member outside the country, they can just sponsor you to come. And when you are a refugee, it's much easier than sending a visa because you can prove you are an asylum seeker, a refugee. And that is how I came. I did not plan to come here; it was not my intention, but because of my life experience, that's how I came here. So it's different than [inaudible] immigrants who plan, who had a plan when they came here. I was just finding safety and a space to stay because I couldn't go back to my country.

In conversations with students in my writing workshop around the theme of torture, Sahra described the harrowing experiences:

> Unless you have lived in a situation of war where you see torture, it is hard to imagine the nightmare. One day your life is fine and you are going to school, and you hear it raining bullets outside and you know that they are executing someone right behind the school door and you have to keep studying. This is a kind of psychological torture that stays with you. But that is what they want, that is how they gain control.

Sahra shared how her brother was diagnosed with PTSD after living though the war, a diagnosis that was difficult for her family to accept initially due to cultural stigma associated with mental illness in Somali culture. She became a strong advocate for her brother to receive help when she arrived in the United States and insisted that her parents get him the treatment he needed. The following transcript begins with Sahra describing a relationship between her experiences as a sister and later, as a mother. Due to the underlying nonlinear storytelling nature of her first language, Sahra's timeline of events may be slightly confusing for readers. The excerpt highlights the complexities of cross-cultural negotiation of meaning; as researchers and cultural brokers, we notice the characteristics of "interlanguage" influences on discourse conventions. Sahra's brother was diagnosed long before her son was born. She explained:

Before I had my son diagnosed, my brother was diagnosed with PTSD and depression. Everything I'm doing right now, everything with my son, started with my brother, and it's more a generational difference—me, who has a child, and my mother, who also has a child, and my brother is the one who got diagnosed first, and I have my son, so the history goes on. So, I have experience with mental illness, and autism as well; it's a different kind of disability. [My brother] was 17 at that time, but that's when he was diagnosed, but the problem started earlier than then. All the signs. Yeah, we were always in Boston, and we never moved to another place. So what I'm saying is, there's a lot of signs, we didn't know how to recognize depression, what it's like. And when we talk about culture, my brother is a boy so the, boys, we are hard on them, you know? We expect them to be strong, not show emotion or nothing. It's seen as a weakness so my mother was pushing him to be, like, "You're the man. You can do this. You know you can fight with this." But, as we know, that's not possible. And I think that adds more problems for my brother. He keeps saying, "Why can't I just make this go away?" He was even hallucinating. And I think those things, if I knew what I know now, that would help earlier on. But we didn't know.

I think the story that happened to my brother was more unique than my son. And the reason I say that is because there's a lot of factors. My parents was older. My mother had my brother when she was 42 years old. And my parents were about to get ready [for] retirement, you know, back when they were—they lost everything. So that put . . . a lot of stress for them to come to a new country with no language and having a young son. They protected my brother so much and give him space and—you know what I mean, right? Many immigrants what they really worry about is that their child might get lost in a different culture, religion, all those things, you know. That protection, they tried to protect him, sometimes is not good for that child because that child needs to fit both worlds. This is his world now and this is where he makes friends and where he's going to live. And they underestimate that in my opinion. So I think because he had experienced civil war and he didn't have that much freedom to explore and he was not one who can—you know, kids are different. For me, I might rebel, but he was like more, you know, they call the good son. Even if he's not happy about it. So I think because of his personality and the age that [it] happened, the civil war, all of those things was different kind of factors. Where we lived at that time, there was no Somali community there, couldn't go to Boston, so we were kind of isolated. Not fit the people we live with, and not live with the people we identify with. So I think that was a lot of issues.

Sahra explained how she learned from these experiences without knowing it, lessons on how to advocate for her own son in the future. In some ways, this experience serving as a cultural mediator and advocate for her brother provided her with experiences that helped her when advocating for her son's rights. Photo 7.2 is one of the still life drawings by Qalid, Sahra's son, that was awarded highest accolades in a high school competition.

Sahra and her parents struggled to learn the language and adapt to the culture when they first came. Sahra explained that she was born around the time that a formal orthography was introduced in Somali, so she had schooling with access to print literacy in her native Somali language. She explains that she also had exposure to schooling in Italian and religious studies in Arabic. It was easier for her to acculturate and acquire English in a print literacy–heavy society like the United States because of her first-language literacy background. She also thinks that her youth was an advantage in her move to the United States as she was not as "set in her ways." In her view, it was much harder for her parents to acculturate because of

**Photo 7.2.
Qalid's
Still Life
Portrait**

both their age but also their limited access to any print literacy, as they were raised at the time when oracy was the primary and preferred mode of communication.

I will never forget one rainy night when Sahra was attending my writing workshop, we were discussing an article about the benefits of anxiety and another about the treatment of immigrants in America. Sahra disputed the author's premise:

> There are different levels of anxiety and stress. In my perspective, there is no benefit of anxiety when it comes to issues of war. People, especially health care professionals who work with immigrants and refugees from these communities, need to understand that. They need to understand our backgrounds, where we are coming from. So, to what you say (referring to another student) and in response to what the author says, the only positive outcome of the anxiety and stress associated with surviving war is the knowledge in life that one day things can be fine and the next day, they can be bad. You develop, if you are lucky, a flexible and adaptable mindset. When Somali immigrants come here, we stand out because of the way we dress, we are Muslim, and the way that we speak. And, we are dark-skinned. In my country, I never referred to myself as a black person. We just were African. We were Somali. I was treated well in my country as a member of the majority population, and now here as a Somali refugee woman, I stand out and people who look like me are treated differently.

This aversion to risk, preparedness for the unpredictable, and adaptability are habits of mind that have helped Sahra to successfully navigate her transition to the United States and to search for the best supports for her son.

RI YAR IYO LIBAAX:
I FELT LIKE A LITTLE GOAT AMONG THE LIONS.

Sahra's fourth son, Qalid, was diagnosed with autism when he was 4½ years old. Sahra realized something was off when she realized that Qalid was not speaking by the age of 3, which she knew because she had three others before Qalid. At first, she struggled to get a diagnosis from the doctors because Qalid seemed physically healthy and was making sounds. They dismissed her worries about Qalid's speech, telling her that he might just be speech-delayed or just confusing the two languages.

> I struggled to diagnose because my son physically look healthy. He was, you know, not talking, but he was making sounds. And when I have concerns and say, "You know what, I don't think my son is talking," the doctor said, "No, no, no, no, he just confused with the two languages." So they were pushing back saying, "Oh, he's going to talk, he's going to talk." I say, "This is not my language. I don't know what this is." They would keep pushing and

saying, "He's going to talk because he's already making sounds." Sometimes, you know, the kid's making the sounds, and they are speech-delayed, and they're speaking more than one language, and they can miss that. They say, "No, no, it's just the second language confusion." And I told them this is my fourth son, I have three other boys. They didn't have no problem with it. Or whatever language we speak at home. So this is different. So they didn't give me the doubt as a mother knowing this is different than the other kids.

STUDENT REFLECTION: Hearing this was a powerful moment, because it really exposed how a doctor's quick dismissal can become a lifelong consequence for families. —Undergraduate student

---

I found this personally surprising coming from my field of TESOL and bilingual education, where we have known in the research for years that bilingualism does not cause speech delays; this is a myth that has long been dispelled. Milestones of pre-language development are the same in all languages. Like other children, most bilingual children speak their first words by age one (e.g., mama, dada). By age 2, most bilingual children can use two-word phrases (e.g., my ball, no juice). These are the same developmental milestones for children who learn only one language. A bilingual toddler might mix parts of a word from one language with parts from another language, but this is not a sign of a language delay due to bilingualism. In fact, this type of code-switching and linguistic transfer is common in bilingual children. While this might make it more difficult for others to understand the child's meaning, it is not a reflection of abnormal or delayed development. The total number of words (the sum of words from both languages the child is learning) should be comparable to the number used by a child the same age speaking one language. If a bilingual child has a speech or language problem, it will show up in both languages. However, these problems are not caused by learning two languages. I wonder why they did not test her son in both languages before jumping to any assumptions. As an ELL consultant in K–12 schools, I have had to dispel this myth to school professionals in countless meetings. Many people still mistakenly believe that bilingualism causes speech delays and as a result, students like Sahra's son may not be appropriately assessed and diagnosed. I tend to see this more in suburban, monolingual spaces like the suburb outside of Boston where Sahra was living at the time. School officials in these contexts tend to have less knowledge of and experience with multilingual populations. Bilingualism should almost never be used as an explanation for speech or language disorder.

Sahra described the meeting with the teachers:

I felt like a little goat among lions. They would not listen to me and I could feel them all looking down on me as if I was not doing something right by my son. I just wanted them to listen and they would not. With all of the teachers and school psychologists against me in the meeting, it felt very condescending and belittling.

When she asked the school for a speech therapist, they tried to make her doubt her decision, saying things like, "Maybe he won't talk at all." The school kept delaying her concerns, so Sahra fought to get an independent education evaluation from the hospital. In this next excerpt, we find another example of the interlanguage complexities involved in the negotiation and clarification of meaning. She explained:

> If you don't have a diagnosis, you don't get the services. Because I didn't agree with the school evaluation and I asked for another second opinion, they asked, "Where'd you like to go?" I said "I'd like to go to the hospital." They say, "Oh, that would be months for waiting!" I just find out. I got it for two weeks.
> *Janet:* You got a visit at the hospital in two weeks?
> *Sahra:* I work in the hospital.
> *Janet:* Oh, I was going to say. I was on the six-month waiting list.
> *Sahra:* I talked with one of the surgeons I work with and he connected me with the other doctors who did the evaluation. Two weeks to the appointment.

Qalid eventually was diagnosed with autism and received an IEP. With services from a speech pathologist and an occupational therapist, "he improved fast. A year later he was talking in full sentences."

Ever the advocate, Sahra critiqued the situation despite Qalid's improvement:

> But another thing I want to emphasize is I'm from another country which, you know, we don't know that much about disability or services available for disability. So I wish I had someone tell me those things. If I wouldn't work in the hospital, I would've never find out. I would just trust whatever the school said. That's how we brought up. The school has the power, you know, the parents don't do anything. Because in Somalia, there's no services. But if I knew the parent rights in special education laws, I would've fight [for] my son even harder than I did. But I didn't know that. I wasn't isolated, which many Somali community are. I wasn't. So I was working in the hospital asking people questions all time and telling them what I need. I was so frustrated because nobody listened. But because I was in that environment, those doctors support me because they teach me what to say. I wish the school would tell me that. All the doctors were the people who tell me these things.

STUDENT REFLECTION: After hearing about how alone and lost they felt at times raising a child with a disability, this struck me as something extremely cruel. In a world where people with disabilities already lack support, this sort of response is disgraceful. —Undergraduate student

---

Fortunately, Sahra had the social capital, knowledge, and wherewithal to advocate for her son's proper diagnosis. She knew, as a mother, that his speech was not developing typically compared to her other sons who were also raised bilingually. Thanks to Sahra's advocacy, he was able to get the diagnosis and the services he needed. In addition, there was an Italian teacher at her son's school who convinced and encouraged her to advocate for her son to get services all the way up to the school superintendent. She did, and the next year her son received services such as 1:1 assistance and speech services.

WAR LA QABO XIISO MA LEH: WHAT IS KNOWN IS NOT INTERESTING.

During our last interview together, Sahra described her son by saying, "My son doesn't fit into the predetermined boxes. What is unknown about him is what makes him so unique." Sahra continued to explain all of the wonderful attributes and talents her son possesses that may be unknown to others but that make him so interesting. She explained that her son was an award-winning and talented high school artist who has received many accolades in high school competitions (see Photo 7.3) in addition to being a top-performing student academically. She described him as friendly, a protective older sibling, and an art aficionado. She explains:

> He's very friendly if he gets to know you, but he doesn't talk that much. He's a very good listener and very helpful. He has a younger brother; he's the best big brother anybody could have. The reason I say he's the best brother, he's

Photo 7.3.
Qalid's Still
Life Two.

always protecting his younger brother. He always makes sure—his younger brother is kind of bossy so, you know, the other boys when he acts like a boss, they might get mad at him, but Qalid, he will talk to him and say, "This is not the right thing to say. What do you want?" You know, he always takes care of him. Makes sure if I argue with him, he will say, "No, no, no, that's not what he meant. He meant this way." So he doesn't like conflict, so he likes to solve the problems. He covers up [for] his brother.

STUDENT REFLECTION: There is always this assumption that a person with a disability can only be a burden to others. I love how his mother clearly destroyed that assumption with this powerful sentence [about being the best big brother]. —Undergraduate student

---

Sahra continued to describe Qalid's networks of support and his protective role of his brother. She proudly explains:

Protection, yeah. I think because his older brothers—I have four [sons] who are very close in age. My oldest son is much older, 6 years apart from the second, so my other boys are like 2 years apart. So the other two I can separate what they do, and him and the little one I cannot separate. So I think while he doesn't always have time to play with his older brothers, this is the closest person he has. He doesn't have a lot of friends. So this is the only person he spends most of his time with.

She further informs us that his circle of friends has expanded as he has grown older and prepares for college and adulthood. He chooses friends with similar interests in art and animation. She explains:

He has more friends now at school, probably two, but friends who are similar to him. My son might be on the spectrum but he's very good at math and science. One of the best in the school. But he shows no interest in pursuing a science degree. He likes the arts. So he and his friends, they draw, engage in animations, and he makes computer programs. That's what he likes, so he only picks friends who have the same interests. And sadly, there are not a lot. And they come over, yes. And he can go to their houses. They paint together. They go to the movies together. He likes anything to do with animation. But they go to the movies. Sometimes they just go to the stores. We have convenience stores everywhere so sometimes they just go around. They take the Orange Line. They go to Boston. I mean the last 2 years he does all that.

Thus Qalid's circle of support includes his friends, his parents, extended family (i.e., grandparents, uncle), and especially his four brothers. It is helpful for school personnel to understand the circles of support for students (and their families)

Photo 7.4. An Example of Art as Voice, Qalid's Design

because it can lead to stronger home–school partnerships, more consistency across home and school settings, and individualized social supports and goals.

Regarding Qalid's interest in art, there is a lot of literature about the power of the arts as a voice for bilingual learners, and I believe the same holds true for students with autism (see Photo 7.4). In terms of language development, when working with emerging bilingual learners, art is a tool that allows students to both express their learning and communicate in the classroom (Wager, Poey, & Berriz, 2017). Research indicates that arts help boost learner confidence and engagement, enhance linguistic and socioemotional development, and promote intercultural awareness and positive cultural identity for emerging bilinguals (Gooden, 2017).

During an interview, Sahra expanded upon this idea of her son's uniqueness. In particular, she described how his uniqueness made his diagnosis complicated:

> So my son, I think he's unique, like anybody else. His uniqueness is even— when he was younger, my son was trouble at school. Number one, he could not communicate, and he was very active. So that put him, you know, caused him a lot of problems with the teachers saying he's not sitting down, he's not doing this. So it's always hearing negatives. Then after a while, he got the speech therapy and he started talking, his behavior subsided and it wasn't as bad as it was. And since then, my son never had a problem one day. They was telling me in the beginning he's not—I have all his IEPs, so they always

telling me like he can't write this, do this, and now they telling me superior, superior. The same kid! That happened.

He still [struggles to speak], you know his tongue is not clear yet. Even though you can understand him, but he doesn't argue. So he just say few words. But, his academic. If you give him this right now this paper, he correct this. Even be able to, this evaluation. He say, "They didn't use this the right way." [Both laughing] You know? So last night we got another letter, we got saying, "This is not right. You see this?" He can see the little things other people don't see it. And spelling, all his brothers they always call him, "What is that word?" He knows. So he's very good in detail and this is the key to what they were telling me he doesn't have no skills with that. But I think sometimes they tell me his weakness is about how he retains information. Like memory. But how can you memorize all of this if you have memory issues? Short memory, long memory, so they talking about the short memory.

ISKAASHATO MA KUFTO:
IF PEOPLE SUPPORT EACH OTHER, THEY DO NOT FALL.

In a full-circle turn of life events, Sahra has decided to pursue a master's degree in Public Health at a local university so she can help other Somali families navigate the challenges of the IEP process and also help enlighten medical professionals about cultural considerations when providing care to Somali families. Ironically, she says, this means she is helping all Somali community members, even those from opposing clans. She wants to help every Somali refugee family within her arm's reach to be informed and avoid the same struggles she encountered with the system. She believes that in sharing her story she will be able to empower and uplift others in her community. She continues to volunteer at the Somali development classes, offering courses to women in her community. She describes her rationale for wanting to share her story:

I think in our Somali community any kind of disability comes with a stigma. So many people they hide. They don't talk about their kids have a disability. Especially if they have a mental [disability]. Even to say my son has IEP some people think that is a sign of weakness so they don't tell that. They might say to the school, I don't want my son or daughter to be in special education, even if the school say that's what your child needs. Just to avoid that labeling. So what I teach parents is there's a time-sensitive [period] your child can benefit in special education.

Sahra mentions that she wants professionals to gain cultural competence and a diversity mindset in which minorities here would be treated with love and sensitivity. She also explains what she thinks medical professionals and educators working with immigrant and refugee families should know:

> I think sometimes it's nice to know family background, where they come from, what are their beliefs. I think sometimes you have to understand in my community if somebody has a mental illness that they go to the hospital they don't say, you know, I have nightmares or any kind of dream; they just talk about physical pain. So to understand that, you know, when they say those things, you don't just talk about the way you have a mental illness. Say the way to support them and let them tell you all the symptoms they have. And I think knowing that background because they're trying to avoid the label, will give you time to make a conclusion. I think understanding other cultures will help. And now we've been here over 20 years. There's a lot of papers written in Somali cultures, their beliefs, and all of those things. And I use those even myself.

While some aspects of the cultural context apply universally to all Somali people, Sahra reminds us of the important differences within countries and even families: "I would say number one, if people still say, 'From same country,' don't generalize them. They have different experience, different background even though they all say Somali or any other country." It is helpful to understand the cultural context, but teachers and other education professionals should also ask questions and get to know each individual family in order to best serve them.

STUDENT REFLECTION: Listening to people's stories always helps me remember how "human" we all are. —Undergraduate student

---

WAXAY ISUGU SOO BIYO SHUBATAY: EVERYTHING COMES TOGETHER.

During our last interview with Sahra, over coffee and cake, it was, coincidentally, Qalid's graduation from high school. She excitedly—and proudly—shared with us her enthusiasm for this milestone and momentous event in her son's journey. Qalid has since been accepted to and is now attending college where he is majoring in Fine Arts.

Our gathering that day between the three of us women, as mothers, researchers, and writers, afforded us a unique opportunity to come together and honor Qalid's accomplishments. We revisited elements of Sahra's family story and took pictures of Qalid's artwork. It was a cathartic time—a time that brought to mind the Somali expression that means "the place at the bottom of the waterfall where the water comes together and settles."

REFLECTION QUESTIONS

- How could educators have prevented Sahra from feeling like "a goat among lions" during Qalid's IEP meetings? What underlying assumptions (about disability, culture, language, and so on) do you think educators held in the meeting with Sahra based on their interactions with her?
- We often hear about the negative aspects (e.g., behavioral challenges, autism epidemic) of autism as a disorder. How did Sahra's description of her son reframe common symptoms associated with autism?
- What cultural assumptions influenced the struggle to diagnose Sahra's brother? How has his example influenced your thinking about engaging with families and teaching students who have survived torture and other trauma?
- How did Sahra finally get the proper diagnosis for her son? In what ways does this portrait shape your understanding of parental advocacy challenges and opportunities among Somali refugee families who have children with disabilities? What are the implications for educators working with these families?
- Reflect on the importance of understanding "interlanguage" and its impact on communicating effectively with bilingual students, parents, or professionals. How might you engage in this cross-cultural negotiation of meaning?

NOTE

1. This is a pseudonym that carries personal and cultural meaning. Bashir is an Arabic name that means "someone who is blessed." Sahra explained that it refers to when it has just rained, the grass is green, and you have everything you need.

REFERENCES

Abdullahi, M. D. (2001). *Culture and customs of Somalia.* Westport, CT: Greenwood Press.

Alitolppa-Niitamo, A. (2001). Liminalities: Expanding and constraining the options of Somali youth in metropolitan Helsinki, Finland. In *Yearbook of Population Research in Finland,* XXXVII (pp. 126–147). Helsinki, Finland: The Population Research Institute.

Alitolppa-Niitamo, A. (2010). The generation in-between: Somali youth and schooling in metropolitan Helsinki. *Intercultural Education, 13*(3), 275–290.

Alitolppa-Niitamo, A., & Abdullahi, A. A. (2002). Somalidiaspora suomessa: Muutoksia, haasteita ja haaveita. (Somali diaspora in Finland: Changes, challenges, and myths). In A. Forsander, E. Ekholm, & P. ym Hautaniemi (Eds.), *Monietnisyys, työ ja yhteiskunta* (pp. 134–147). Helsinki, Finland: Palmenia-kustannus.

Boyle, E., & Ali, A. (2010). Culture, structure, and the Somali refugee experience in Somali immigrant family transformation. *International Migration, 48*, 47–49.

Cavallera, V., Reggi, M., Abdi, S., Jinnah, Z., Kivelenge, J., Warsame, A. M., Yusuf, A. M., & Ventevogel, P. (2016). *Culture, context and mental health of Somali refugees: A primer for staff working in mental health and psychosocial support programmes.* United Nations High Commissioner for Refugees.

Gooden, A. (2017). Reach for the stars: Restructuring schooling for emergent bilinguals with a whole-child, arts-infused curricular approach. *Journal of Pluralism, Pedagogy, and Practice, 9(1)*, 168–196.

Harris, H. (2004). The Somali community in the UK: What we know and how we know it. Retrieved from www.icar.org/uk/download.php?id=67

Hasnain, R., Cohon Shaikh, L., & Shanawani, H. (2008). Disability and the Muslim perspective: An introduction for rehabilitation and health care providers. *Center for International Rehabilitation Research Information and Exchange.* Buffalo, NY: The State University of New York Press.

Hawley, G. (2019, July 24). *Ambivalent nativism, Trump supporters' attitudes towards Islam and Muslim immigration.* Brookings Institution Report. Retrieved from www.brookings.edu/research/ambivalent-nativism-trump-supporters-attitudes-toward-islam-and-muslim-immigration/

Hesse, B. (2010). Introduction: The myth of Somali. *Journal of Contemporary African Studies,28*(3), 247–259

Hofstede, G. (2011). Dimensionalizing cultures: The Hofstede model in context. *Online Readings in Psychology and Culture, 2*(1). Retrieved from doi.org/10.9707/2307-0919.1014.

Kapchits, G. (1998). The Somali oral traditions: A call for salvation. In W. Heissig & R. Schott (Eds.), *Die heutige Bedeutung oraler Traditionen [The Present-Day Importance of Oral Traditions].* Abhandlungen der Nordrhein-Westfälischen Akademie der Wissenchaften, vol. 102. VS Verlag für Sozialwissenschaften.

Lewis, I. (2008). *Understanding Somalia and Somaliland: Culture, history, society.* New York, NY: Columbia University Press.

Lustig, A., & Koehster, J. (2017). *Intercultural competence: Interpersonal communication across cultures* (8th ed.). New York, NY: Pearson.

Niayesh, V. (2019, September 26). Trump's travel ban really was a Muslim ban, data suggests. *The Washington Post.* Retrieved from www.washingtonpost.com/politics/2019/09/26/trumps-muslim-ban-really-was-muslim-ban-thats-what-data-suggest/

Rohwerder, B. (2018). *Disability in Somalia.* K4D Helpdesk Report. Brighton, UK: Institute of Development Studies.

Sida. (2014). *Disability rights in Somalia.* Retrieved from www.sida.se/globalassets/sida/eng/partners/human-rights-basedapproach/disability/rights-of-persons-with-disabilities-somalia.pdf

Starck, J. (2016). *Somalian families' views on disabled children and Finnish health care services* [Master's thesis]. Laurea University of Applied Sciences, Helsinki, Finland.

United Nations High Commission for Refugees (UNHCR). (2003). Somali Bantus leave for America with hopes for a new life. Retrieved from www.unhcr.org/news/NEWS/3eccda802.html

Wager, A. C., Poey, V. M., & Berriz, B. R. (2017). Art as voice: Creating access for emergent bilingual learners. *Journal of Pedagogy, Pluralism, and Practice, 9*(1), full issue. Retrieved from https://digitalcommons.lesley.edu/jppp/vol9/iss1/1.

CHAPTER 8

Knowledge to Action
Enacting Cultural Humility

We have long known about the value of family engagement and culturally responsive practices for leading to improved outcomes for children. Both areas of research emphasize the importance of moving practitioners from a deficit-oriented perspective to an asset-based approach. Similarly, our use of Disability Studies in Education (DSE) theory and portraiture methodology position culturally and linguistically diverse (CLD) families as offering intrinsic value to the field of special education and to the work of service providers for children labeled with disabilities. These areas of research and practice are interconnected; DSE theory and what we learned about cultural humility informed our choice of portraiture method for engaging CLD families for this book.

In Chapter 1 we explained the distinction between cultural competence and cultural humility, preferring to use the latter term because it emphasizes the *ongoing process of learning* rather than suggesting that we learn a limited set of facts that make us competent. Preservice professionals who will be working with CLD families with children with disabilities, as well as professionals currently working with those families, need many opportunities to continually learn about themselves, about others' positionality, and the myriad ways to engage families with cultural humility. Our book offers you, our readers, many such opportunities to learn from these six CLD families about their cultural perspectives on the experience of schooling their children. As noted previously and repeatedly, none of the families represents a singular, monolithic group identity. Instead, each of these family stories is unique, complex, and limited to what was shared and by the perspectives of those of us who composed the portraits. Each portrait provides insight into a variety of issues that many families of children with disabilities experience. By assembling these portraits together, we found a deeper understanding of the reasons behind what might otherwise be viewed by preservice teachers and school professionals as confusing or problematic behavior on behalf of families. Instead of focusing on what might be challenging circumstances, we hope these layered co-constructed portraits, crafted through an iterative process of cultural brokering, illustrate the many talents and valuable local knowledge of CLD families.

As professors working in teacher education programs, we notice few current materials and resources that we can use to help prepare our university students for developing understanding of families of disabled children of immigrant and/

or refugee families living in the United States. We knew we could not fill this gap without learning more about the experiences of local families. Our 5-year multifaceted research project involved collaborating with several CLD families in a variety of ways: serving as guest speakers (i.e., they were guest speakers in our courses and we were guest speakers at their parent groups), volunteering at community and cultural events, presenting at conferences and workshops, conducting research, organizing focus groups, and writing. There were many families with whom we worked whose stories are not included in this book for a variety of reasons: some did not have the time or financial resources; others withdrew for fear of retaliation by school personnel; and still others simply did not respond to our requests. Although we included only six family stories, what we learned from the other families and adults with disabilities who visited our classes undoubtedly informed our project.

Affirming disability and forging connections with CLD families often requires fundamental changes to one's attitudes and assumptions about others. Perspective-taking emerged as valuable for developing our students' understanding of families' point of view. Our students repeatedly wrote about the positive impact of these interactions and how we established an expectation that, as one student put it, "We look at everything in terms of all these different identity categories. Perspective and understanding others' perspectives was super important to this class." Additionally, parents sometimes expressed the importance of perspective taking by school professionals related to their children. In her portrait (Chapter 4), María suggests that teachers would better understand her son's so-called misbehavior if they would "get in his shoes"; that his behavior is his form of communication in which he was seeking more support. While each of the family stories in this volume are unique, their stories shed light on the impact of systemic inequities of practice often fraught with cultural misunderstandings.

Cultural misunderstandings take many forms, from what may be thought of as a well-intentioned comment to broader systems based on policies that disempower many families who are already marginalized by social responses to their perceived minoritized statuses. For example, the speech language pathologist (SLP) in Tiny's IEP meeting (Chapter 3), from Oanh's perspective, dismissed her inquiry and implied an inability to learn how to encode her daughter's augmentative communication device. In a society that is ableist and racist, people who are not White and able-bodied are not perceived as just different, but deficient. Further, these families described "a system" indifferent to their customs and values.

The American special education process is organized in a way that requires parent advocacy, an added expectation of labor on the part of many immigrant families to learn not just a new set of specialized vocabulary but also a completely separate process from that of the "typical" American approach to schooling in "general education." This supplemental work for ethnic majority families has been documented for years and has been implicated in research about racial, cultural, and economic disparities (Kalyanpur, Harry, & Skrtic, 2000). While we did not focus our analysis on gender roles, these portraits all relied on the perspectives and labor of women of color. As described in Chapter 1, this labor of writing, meeting for interviews, editing, and checking for understanding was *in addition to* the labor involved with managing the communication with many other professionals to coordinate services for their own children, often in their second or third language. Oanh Bui's portrait includes a graphic organizer illustrating the complex coordination of Tiny's care (Chapter 3), an experience shared by many families. Additionally, the emotional work of retelling their experiences, some of which were upsetting, contributed to the labor expected—and embraced—by each of these women.

These portraits also illustrate the importance of understanding that there are subtleties of difference within cultural groups. For example, Susan Ou and Oanh Bui (Chapters 2 and 3, respectively) explained the difference between direct translation of spoken dialects or written language, and interpretation of meaning behind the words used in the special education referral, assessment, and service delivery models. They point out that if the parents do not understand the meaning behind the words in an Individualized Education Program (IEP) outlining special education services, their signed consent is disingenuous at best and meaningless at worst. They advocate for increasing the number of bilingual professionals, especially interpreters and speech language pathologists trained in special education and expanding the practice of using cultural brokers. Their stories were shared as parents, but also as cultural brokers themselves with many years of experience working with other Asian immigrant families. Sahra's story (Chapter 7) provides yet another example of the differences within cultural groups when she describes the social hierarchies between the nomadic Bantu and her own subculture of Somalis of Cushitic descent. Somali Bantus are ethnically, physically, and culturally distinct from indigenous Somalis of Cushitic descent, and they have remained marginalized ever since their arrival in Somalia. Punita (Chapter 5), too, emphasized the importance of developing an understanding of the subtleties of differences between the Indian diaspora.

These portraits illustrate the broad and lasting impact of school recommendations. Although we assume the intent of the school professionals was to bring about only positive outcomes for the children with disabilities, some recommendations were shortsighted, based on misinformation, or simply ethnocentric and prejudicial. The SLP in Tiny's IEP meeting discouraged her mother Oanh from teaching her daughter Vietnamese (Chapter 3), and the SLP in Sachin's IEP meeting told his parents not to speak Hindi in their home (Chapter 5). Though Oanh resisted the professional's advice and taught herself how to incorporate Vietnamese into Tiny's AAC device, Sachin's parents acquiesced to the opinion of the speech language pathologist. These recommendations had lifelong and extensive impact on both families. Sachin and his brothers grew up without learning their parents' or grandparents' first language. Since they did not learn the family tongue, their communication and relationships with their paternal grandparents and extended family was limited when they visited India as young adults.

In Chapter 5, Sachin's mother, Punita, described her perspective of having a son diagnosed with autism living in the Midwest. Their painful experience with one school brings attention to the highly controversial—and we think reprehensible—use of restraint and seclusion, a practice known to be disproportionately used with students of color (see Abamu & Manning, 2019). While Punita had the cultural and social capital to complain to the administration and subsequently remove her son from the school, this is not the case for many families. She somewhat reluctantly shared the "duct tape story" because just the memory of the incident brought up strong emotions. However, she hopes that talking about it brings awareness and could lead to systematic changes and the elimination of corporal punishment in schools.

These families want to hold the school system and the professionals accountable for their recommendations. Sahra (Chapter 7) believes that if she had not challenged the professionals' opinion, her son would not have received the services he needed to develop the skills necessary for successfully completing his formal schooling. For Kimiya's sister, Samin (Chapter 6), it is less clear who might be held to account for the school's decision not to provide her with communication supports and services, such as augmentative alternative communication (AAC). While Oanh (Chapter 3) advocated with the school and worked tirelessly at home to promote Tiny's communication skills through her use of AAC, Tiny continues to face barriers to using her AAC at school and in the community. María (Chapter 4) encountered the all-too-common barriers of language access (i.e., materials not translated into Spanish, lack of a professional interpreter at meetings) during Juan's IEP meetings. These are basic problems that not only are illegal, but also should be easily addressed. Additionally, she dealt with teachers who held low expectations for Juan based on their (mis)interpretation of his behaviors, rather than teaching and supporting him in inclusive ways so that he would not engage in those behaviors.

PERSONAL ACTION PLAN FOR CHANGE

In this section, we offer professionals and university students an opportunity to think about how to apply the insights from the six portraits. Several of our students who meet with guest speakers in our classes (like those featured in the portraits), or who engage in community-based field experiences interacting with CLD people with disabilities and their families, have used the following guiding questions as they progress through the preservice program. We developed a sample Action Plan alongside two cultural brokers for an article published in a practitioner journal (see Rossetti, Sauer, Bui, & Ou, 2017). The Action Plan format we share in this chapter is an expanded version from the same model; although here we refer to Susan's family portrait, you could use any of the portrait chapters, or any family with whom you work. This Action Plan discussion is intended to be useful as a guide for the changes in your own practices to better collaborate with CLD families and better support their children with disabilities. We suggest you act proactively and purposefully. Embrace Susan Ou's advice to "do your research"; learn about the general cultural backgrounds of your students' families, and their unique histories, values, and perspectives about disability. Practice cultural humility and develop your own cultural brokering skills by forging those connections referred to by Sara Lawrence-Lightfoot (Chapter 1) and described by Sachin Arora (Chapter 5). There are three steps, or guiding questions, outlined in the Action Plan: (1) How culturally responsive am I?; (2) Who is the family of focus?; and (3) How can we develop a more collaborative relationship with this family?

How Culturally Responsive Am I?

We encourage you to take time for personal reflection about your own positionality, at different points in time. Since everyone has a dynamic sense of identity depending on time, location, and situation, reading these family stories provides an opportunity to revisit this question. Similarly, every time you meet a new student and his or her family, you have an opportunity to "check in with yourself." There are many resources for this process. Banks (2006) describes several "microcultures" that influence our development of a "cultural stance." These microcultures could include your ethnic group, race, social class, gender, region, religion, and disability status. Georgetown University's National Center for Cultural Competence (nccc.georgetown.edu/) provides online self-assessments we used ourselves. The goal of engaging in this process is to build a sense of what Tervalon and Murray-Garcia (1998) refer to as *cultural humility*, "a communal reflection" originally used to examine health disparities and institutional inequities. In the video "Cultural Humility: People, Principles and Practices" (melanietervalon.com/wp-content/uploads/2013/08/Cultural-Humility-A-Video.pdf), Tervalon and Murray-Garcia explain how this daily reflective practice repositions care providers as lifelong learners, and students of their clients and patients.

There are a variety of resources that may be useful for examining one's own social identities that can also be helpful in developing knowledge about broader social inequities. In one preservice teacher program, Brown, Vesely, and Dallman (2016) found the combination of a self-assessment inventory, case studies, and role-playing scenarios were effective in facilitating discussions about implicit bias and stereotypes when engaging CLD families. Similar to some of our work, they also embraced the notion of cultural humility. Diane Goodman's framework, Cultural Competence for Social Justice (2013), offers another tool we have used with our preservice students. She writes:

> Cultural competence for social justice is the ability to live and work effectively in culturally diverse environments and enact a commitment to social justice. Social justice refers to creating a society (or community, organization, or campus) with an equitable

distribution of resources and opportunities. . . . [This] model can help us navigate the path towards greater understanding, effectiveness, equity, and inclusion. (p. 1)

Goodman recognizes that social identities interact to shape people's sense of themselves and their experiences, with five key components: (1) self-awareness, (2) understanding and valuing others, (3) knowledge of societal inequities, (4) skills to interact effectively with a variety of people in different contexts, and (5) skills to foster equity and inclusion (pp. 1–3).

Since the university where one author (Janet) teaches adopted Goodman's framework, she asked her students to use Goodman's framework to identify events, people, readings, or critical incidents they thought influenced their positionality, knowledge of societal oppressions, or development of interpersonal skills for interacting with a diversity of people to foster equity at personal or institutional levels. The students became increasingly adept at identifying their positionality and privileges. They seemed to understand the complexity of the work. Students described several examples of critical incidents during their internships and class discussions, but most often their responses mention a personal story as having the greatest impact on their understanding of others' marginalized experiences.

One graduate student working with the other author (Zach) described various aspects to her identity as Latinx:

> For many Latinx people, the country/land their family or themselves come from has a strong weight in their identity. Each country or region of Latin America has its own cultural norms, language, foods, music, dances, history of oppressing and being oppressed, etc. In the context of the United States, that part of our identity is stripped away and narrowed down to a single concept. By labeling people with just one term, you eliminate the complexity of the in-group dynamics.
>
> Many Latinx people are multilingual. Within their knowledge of languages, there exists many dialects. For example, growing up in Miami, I spoke Spanglish (a mix of English and Spanish) and Argentinian Spanish with my family, Argentinian Spanish with my friends, and English at school. Now, living in Boston, I speak formal Spanish at work, formal English at school, Spanglish with my partner, and Argentinian Spanish with my family. Contexts at times force us to code-switch and limit our ability to fully express ourselves.
>
> Within Latinx culture, language is used to oppress smaller minority groups. Spanish is one of the most widely spoken [languages] by Latinx people. Spanish carries the strong weight of sexism. Binaries rule the language; a/o shape almost all nouns. Whenever there is a group of people and there is one person who is perceived to be male, the plural nouns always end in "o" the male form. For those who speak the most accepted/academic form of Spanish, their knowledge is an asset. For those who speak any

other language that is not the one accepted by White culture, their language becomes a point of oppression.

This student selected several quotes from published work to illustrate the impact of immigration, language, race, and other aspects of identity. One quote, by criminal justice researcher Nicole Gonzalez Van Cleve (2016), highlights how different perspectives influence interpretations and values: "It is a deficit when you speak Spanish, but it's an asset to Whites and White Americans when they speak it. This is the ultimate form of exclusion."

One aspect of our multifaceted project involved examining these attitudinal changes among our university preservice social and education professionals. We wanted to know if the opportunity to learn more about and from people with disabilities and their families met course outcomes related to developing empathy. Empathy, along with attitudes of curiosity and respect, are thought to be important for negotiating cross-cultural interactions (Georgetown University National Center for Cultural Competency, n.d.). Using the work of social scientist Brené Brown (2008) and others (Bloom, 2016; Van Der Klift & Kunc, 2019), Marsh (2019) studied a sampling of our university students' written work to identify examples of empathy. Notably, Brown (2008) differentiates empathy from sympathy; while both are considered affective dispositions, *sympathy* is when someone feels sorry for another person, whereas *empathy* is described as feeling similarly to another person. In other words, sympathy reflects a deficit orientation, while empathy promotes a strengths-based reframing of disability. Marsh (2019) discusses some of the complications associated with empathy:

> Bloom (2016) suggests that affective empathy along with rational (i.e., reasoned) compassion more reliably leads to better moral judgment, and ultimately social justice. As far as sympathy and pity, Bloom views these as only negative, arguing that there is no positive emotion that can be held up as an example of sympathy or pity (p. 40). Kunc and Van Der Klift (2019) maintain that sympathy and prejudice can co-exist, resulting in frustrating interactions in which persons with disabilities are "helped" in a fashion more akin to humiliating than to humaneness. Similarly, Diane Goodman (2000) points out the paradox of people of privilege who empathize and as a result equate the experiences of individuals from marginalized groups with their own, discounting their own social location and access to dominant power structures. (Marsh, 2019, p. 4)

Marsh (2019) agrees with Bloom's (2016) idea that people progress from affective (feelings), to cognitive (thinking), to behavioral (action) notions of empathy. Since we did not assess our students' actions, we relied upon their written work as our data sources for analysis. The data included students' papers, course evaluations, and reflections following an event. Using Batson's (2011) forms of empathy to distinguish between students' cognitive versus aesthetic (projecting oneself into another person's situation) versus projective (role-taking) empathy, Marsh found that all of the students wrote about their empathy for the people they directly interacted with, and concluded that perspective shifting "boosts" empathy, and empathy develops understanding and perspective taking.

Who Is This Family?

As with building cultural understanding, there are many resources and frameworks based on decades of research into family dynamics. Regardless of the approach or tools you use to develop your understanding of a family, we cannot overemphasize the value of, as Susan said, "doing your research" about the family's culture. To help you learn, we suggest you make use of local cultural brokers (Jezewski & Sotnik, 2001). Cultural brokers can help professionals begin to learn general and more nuanced cultural communication norms, the family members' attitudes toward disability markers, and which language(s) the family may prefer to use when seeking out local resources and information about the special education process. Whereas Susan (Chapter 2), Oanh (Chapter 3), and Olga (Chapter 4) held official positions as "cultural outreach brokers," Maureen (Chapter 4), Punita (Chapter 5), Kimiya (Chapter 6), and Amy (Chapter 7) all enacted cross-cultural brokering in the writing of these portrait narratives. We (Janet and Zach) also enacted cultural brokering as we negotiated meanings within and across contexts in order to facilitate the data collection and co-construction of the portraits amid possible tensions of power and privilege.

We also encourage reading about the family dynamics from those who have lived through it as the subject of the process. Autobiographies written by self-advocates are increasingly available. For instance, Hinkle (2019), a doctoral student, writes:

> Students and parents can design IEPs with a strengths-based focus when it comes to student's needs and goals. To do so, start by making a list of everything positive about the child, including their gifts, strengths, talents, and interests and all positive achievements the child has done, both academically and socially. Think about what that child brings to the classroom that they can offer to a teacher and their classmates. (para 5)

Hinkle describes a specific approach for not only reframing disability from a deficit orientation to a strengths-based one, but for repositioning students with disabilities and their families as central actors in the IEP process.

One useful framework for conceptualizing and working with families of children with disabilities is the Resilience Model (Kochhar-Bryant, 2008), which outlines five "stages" family members might move through: identification of disability, self-education, reflection about self and family, advocacy and empowerment, and appreciation and enlightenment. This model emphasizes family strengths, especially their ability to adapt to the life changes that occur when disability enters the family unit. It also inherently recognizes that while disability is often unexpected, it is not a tragedy resulting in deficit only. Several family systems and ecological theories have been developed that readers might also find useful (Ferguson, 2002;

Lareau, 2011; Turnbull, Turnbull, Erwin, Soodak, & Shogren, 2011), keeping in mind that what constitutes a family is based on socially, culturally, and historically situated circumstances.

Our students were invited to respond to the question "Who is this family?" after having met with Susan (and all of the other family participants). They were taught about portraiture and invited to write their own mini-portrait papers. When focusing on Susan's older son, rather than starting with a clinical, diagnostic label, one student began her writing response by describing the family this way:

> Susan shows a playful image of her son, Bruce, who she says loves balls, Curious George, and cards. At that time Bruce was just shy of 3 years old, and he attended day care at a center where English, Mandarin, and Cantonese were all spoken. At home, the family spoke predominantly Cantonese and limited English.

The college student also identified the child's strengths as described in the preschool's assessment (his curiosity and his cooperation), before summarizing the (deficit-oriented) qualities that overshadowed the special education report. We encourage our students to identify a child's strengths and interests while considering the whole child (see Kluth & Dimon-Borowski, 2003) and the child's relationships to his family, peers, and other people in his Circle of Friends (Falvey, Forest, Pearpoint, & Rosenberg, 1997). Their publishers' website (Inclusion.com) explains, "Circles of Friends or Circles of Support have been in every society since the dawn of time. . . . [It] is not a program. It is a way of living. It has an underlying philosophy of interdependence." Newton and Wilson (2003) describe Circle of Friends as a process of mobilizing peers of a young person with a disability to help problem-solve and provide support. On their website (inclusive-solutions.com/circles/circle-of-friends/what-is-a-circle-of-friends/) they quote the poet Ted Hughes, who described one's support group as akin to "a shared bank account of the group wealth." This practice of identifying who the people are in a child's life can help develop a richer understanding of a child's family, and their cultural wealth.

In addition to developing an understanding of a family, we realize that our preservice teachers need to learn how to navigate and work within the education system and become adept at its professional discourse. For example, this undergraduate student's paper showed her growing understanding of the complexity of language acquisition:

> As a multilingual child with English as a second language, many of the behaviors and challenges he was facing were typical of a child exposed to many different languages at once. For multilingual children like Bruce, a "silent period" and "code-switching" are considered common. *Code-switching* is when the child is hearing a language and needs to internally determine which language is being spoken in order to process and respond.

The *silent period* is when a child who is exposed to multiple languages has limited speech because they are focusing on learning the different languages they are being exposed to. The team decided Bruce needed more time to develop his speech and language in multiple languages than his monolingual peers needed to develop proficiency in communication for children in early childhood settings.

Our university students, and others interested in engaging with CLD families in the schooling process, clearly need more time to develop a complex understanding of their intersecting identities, values, and perspectives. We know the challenges of working in schools, and with families, but have found that the time taken to more fully learn about each child's family in the process of developing these relationships is always worthwhile, and essential for doing this work.

How Can We Develop a More Collaborative Relationship with This Family?

CLD families, like all families, want to be treated with respect. Sometimes the starting point for school professionals is to be more patient and respectful when interacting with all families. Susan's story provides readers with many possibilities for school professionals working with either of her boys to develop a more collaborative relationship with the family. One can easily start by following her advice to "Do your research." Use the Internet to start exploring general information about—in the case of Ian and Bruce's family—China, its history, and its various languages and cultural groups. Find out about community cultural events to see about attending—there's something powerful about spending time in places outside your own comfort zone. Our students who joined us at the Lunar New Year consistently report how much they learned and enjoyed themselves. Identify a local Chinese cultural broker to ask questions; ask the family questions to find out about their language and culture; and see if you can learn how they perceive the concept of disability, their goals for their child, their expectations for school, and so on. Try learning a greeting in the family's home language, in this case, in Cantonese. Families might also share explanations of their chosen names.

In preparation for the next IEP meeting, consider the meeting logistics such as scheduling at times when Susan and her husband are not working and when they have child care. Ensure that all materials are translated beforehand, including information about their child(ren)'s disabilities, and have a professional interpreter with experience in special education come prepared. You will also need to schedule the meeting to be longer when you have an interpreter. Although Susan herself is a cultural broker who has years of experience working with schools, do not make assumptions that she, and the other family members, understand the intricacies of every step in the special education process. We will be the first to admit that even with our own extensive knowledge, no one knows everything about every aspect of each decision that needs to be made in an IEP meeting. Services and personnel change as well, so be sure to explain each consideration. Remember that the advocacy expectation in U.S. special education runs counter to Chinese cultural norms, so if Susan's family asks a question or for a service, it likely is a hard thing to do. Refer the family to the local Parent Training and Information Center (PTI) by giving them the name and number of a particular person who you've found has knowledge of Chinese culture; after explaining explicitly the school's expectations, tell them that the PTI can help advocate on their behalf.

During the meeting you might remind yourself that if they nod in response to a suggestion, it does not mean they agree; it's best to give families time to consider their options, not to rush, if the ideal of home–school collaboration with parent participation is to be realized. Work to maintain harmony in the meeting/process even when negotiating or disagreeing about appropriate services; use conflict resolution strategies, but also a culturally relevant approach to ensure that the family can convey what they want and not just agree to avoid conflict. Also, be sure to follow up with them after the meeting, offering another opportunity to build trust and shared understanding. Remember, Susan said the Chinese families she works with seek face-to-face communication as much as possible.

According to the Department of Education, data regarding students who are English language learners (ELLs) who were also determined to be entitled to special education services is highly variable, depending on the sources and location. "In the 2011–2012 school year, data collected from special education programs in each state indicated that ELLs represented anywhere from 0% to 31% of students with disabilities, ages 6 through 21" (Liu, Ward, Thurlow, & Christensen, 2017, p. 553). Researchers in the field of ELL and disability have long argued that language acquisition can take longer than the time many districts provide for them to develop academic proficiency, particularly in expressive forms of communication (Serpa, 2019; Slama et al., 2017). This issue might be one reason for the discrepancy.

The United States is experiencing another wave of immigrants, and as educators, our role is ensuring their success. The first of many recommendations to administrators aiming to support their faculty, according to researchers Stepanek, Raphael, Autio, Deussen, and Thompson (2010), is to "make success for ELLs a central issue." Preservice student teachers familiar with Susan's story (or experiences of other bi/multilingual families whose children were diagnosed with disabilities) were asked to find research-based strategies and recommendations they might suggest for Susan's (or other) children. Here are some of our students' research suggestions:

Herrell and Jordan's (2016) *Fifty Strategies for Teaching English Language Learners* emphasizes the importance of using real objects (over photographs) to teach content, providing learners with as much sensory information as possible. Santillan, Jacobs, and Wright (2015) assert that physical education (PE) instruction naturally provides ELL students with authentic and interactive learning opportunities. Depending on the individual students' needs, teachers would have to consider assistive technologies for mobility adaptations to ensure access. Santillan and colleagues point out that like other school subjects, in PE there are many vocabulary terms and concepts (special materials, games), so specific language objectives are necessary to include in lesson planning. They suggest labeling equipment and using teacher modeling and videos (always use Closed Captioning for all videos). Carr (2012) suggests teachers combine using the following reading strategies all together: cues, KWL, visuals, think-pair-share, think aloud, and summarization.

Miller (2016) says that one of the most important techniques when teaching ELLs identified as having learning disabilities is contextualizing the instruction. "There are three steps to provide culturally responsive instructional strategies . . . (a) building vocabulary, (b) building background, and (c) providing ample opportunities to practice and apply the information that the students have been taught" (p. 59). Miller explains that when he says "multiple opportunities," he means students need as many as 12–16 "exposures" in a variety of situations to acquire new vocabulary. These "exposures," or opportunities to acquire a second language, should include explicit instruction and could involve the use of concept maps and visual mnemonics. Explicit instruction that shows a visual connection to cognates in a student's home language has shown to be effective.

Since we know that meaningful communication and peer interactions can serve as powerful motivation for language learning, we were pleased to read the following recommendation for Susan's younger son, Ian, from one of our undergraduate students:

> One strategy that may help Ian with his language development would be to incorporate a social group into his daily routine. This group could be within the classroom or outside of it, and topic of discussion could be related to class topics or general topics outside of class. Research has shown the students who are given opportunities to engage in critical and cognitive thinking through conversations with peers in either their first or second language have greater skills in vocabulary usage (Rance-Roney, 2008). Given that Ian has difficulty in utilizing his vocabulary in both his native and his second language, taking part in a social group in either or both of his languages would allow him the space to use his language and develop familiarity with vocabulary usage.
>
> Stemming from this, Ian would likely benefit from integrated bilingual education in and out of the classroom. It's been shown that bilingual students who have quality oral language exposure in their native language develop their vocabulary knowledge and usage better in that native language (Gamez & Levine, 2013).

In addition to the benefits of language development (in multiple languages), the natural supports and inclusive opportunities of social groups also result in improvements of social belonging and in the quantity and quality of social interactions experienced by students with disabilities. This is a critical consideration for school personnel because friendships between students with and without intellectual and developmental disabilities (IDD) remain infrequent (Petrina, Carter, & Stephenson, 2014; Tipton, Christensen, & Blacher, 2013). A growing body of research indicates that opportunity barriers (i.e., infrequent or ineffective social interaction opportunities, thus limited opportunities to build relationships with peers without IDD) may play a more prominent role in friendship development than the social skills of students with IDD (Kalymon, Gettinger, & Hanley-Maxwell, 2010; Rossetti, Ross, & Brennen, 2017). Multiple studies have indicated that increased social opportunities (e.g., shared learning tasks, more time with peers, and decreased adult proximity) in inclusive settings that become consistent over time can lead to higher-quality social interactions and ultimately to the development of friendships between students with and without IDD (Rossetti, Ross, & Brennen, 2017).

CONCLUSION

Universities are beginning to respond to students' calls for acknowledging intersectionality and creating more interdisciplinary courses to meet the demands of an increasingly diverse school context. Disability Studies in Education programs can now be found at many IHEs across the United States and abroad that offer preservice professionals with opportunities for developing greater understanding of the social, cultural, historical, and political influences on the special education system. Our use of the DSE theoretical framework to approach our work with CLD families highlights issues of power and social hierarchies involved in the process of assessment, determining eligibility, and decisions regarding service delivery for children and youth entitled to a free and equitable education. We hope the immigrant family experiences described in this book will be used for critical reflection by those of us responsible for supporting the education of children and youth in our care. We think knowledge is power, but action is needed, especially "in these perilous times" Lawrence-Lightfoot (2017).

REFERENCES

Abamu, J., & Manning, R. (2019). Desperation and broken trust: When schools restrain students or lock them in rooms. Retrieved from www.npr.org/2019/06/05/726519409/desperation-and-broken-trust-when-schools-restrain-students-or-lock-them-in-room

Banks, J. (2006). *Cultural diversity and education: Foundations, curriculum, and teaching* (5th ed.). Boston, MA: Allyn & Bacon.

Batson, C. D. (2011). These things called empathy: Eight related but distinct phenomena. In J. Decety & W. Ickes (Eds.), *The social neuroscience of empathy* (pp. 3–15). Cambridge, MA: MIT Press.

Bloom, P. (2016). *Against empathy: The case for rational compassion.* New York, NY: Harper Collins.

Brown, B. (2008). *I thought it was just me (but it isn't): Making the journey from "what will people think?" to "I am enough."* New York, NY: Random House.

Brown, E. L., Vesely, C. K.., & Dallman, L. (2016). Unpacking biases: Developing cultural humility in early childhood and elementary teacher candidates. *Teacher Educators' Journal, 9* (75–96).

Carr, J. (2012, October 25). Strategies for teaching English learners and students with learning disabilities. *ASCD Express, 8*(2). Retrieved from www.ascd.org/ascd-express /vol8/802-carr.aspx

Falvey, M., Forest, M., Pearpoint, J., & Rosenberg, R. (1997). *All my life's a circle—Using the tools: Circles, maps & paths.* Toronto, Canada: Inclusion Press.

Ferguson, P. (2002). A place in the family: An historical interpretation of research on parental reactions to having a child with a disability. *Journal of Special Education, 36*(3), 124–147. doi:10.1177/00224669020360030201

Gamez, P. B., & Levine, S. C. (2013). Oral language skills of Spanish-speaking English language learners: The impact of high-quality native language exposure. *Applied Psycholinguistics, 34*, 673–696.

Georgetown University National Center for Cultural Competence (NCCC). (n.d.). *Foundations of cultural & linguistic competence.* Washington, DC: Georgetown University Center for Child & Human Development. Retrieved from nccc.georgetown.edu /foundations/

Gonzalez Van Cleve, N. (2016). *Crook county: Racism and injustice in America's largest criminal court.* Stanford, CA: Stanford University Press.

Goodman, D. J. (2000). Motivating people from privileged groups to support social justice. *Teachers College Record, 102*(6), 1061–1085.

Goodman, D. J. (2013). Cultural competency for social justice [Blog post]. Retrieved from acpacsje.wordpress.com/2013/02/05/cultural-competency-for-social-justice-by-diane -j-goodman-ed-d/

Herrell, A., & Jordan, M. (2016). *Fifty strategies for teaching English language learners* (5th ed.). Upper Saddle River, NJ: Pearson.

Hinkle, S. (2019, May 20). Navigating the special education system with a disability studies lens [blog post]. Retrieved from https://blogs.chapman.edu/tpi/2019/05/20/ navigating-the-special-education-system-with-a-disability-studies-lens-part-1/

Jezewski, M. A., & Sotnik, P. (2001). *Culture brokering: Providing culturally competent rehabilitation services to foreign-born persons.* Buffalo, NY: Center for International Rehabilitation Research Information and Exchange (CIRRIE). Retrieved from cirrie-sphhp .webapps.buffalo.edu/culture/monographs/cb.php

Kalyanpur, M., Harry, B., & Skrtic, T. (2000). Equity and advocacy expectations of culturally diverse families' participation in special education. *International Journal of Disability, Development and Education, 47*, 119–136.

Kalymon, K., Gettinger, M., & Hanley-Maxwell, C. (2010). Middle school boys' perspectives on social relationships with peers with disabilities. *Remedial and Special Education, 31*, 305–316. doi:10.1177/0741932508327470

Kluth, P., & Dimon-Borowski, M (2003). Strengths and strategies profile form. Retrieved from www.paulakluth.com/readings/inclusive-schooling/strengths-and-strategies/

Kochhar-Bryant, C. (2008). *Collaboration and system coordination from early childhood to post-high school.* Englewood Cliffs, NJ: Prentice Hall-Merrill Education Publishers.

Lareau, A. (2011). *Unequal childhoods: Class, race, and family life.* Berkeley, CA: University of California Press.

Lawrence-Lightfoot, S. (2017, April 28). *"Let the great brown river smile." Liberating frames and educational discourses: On view, voice, and visibility.* Distinguished Lecture presented at the annual meeting of the American Educational Research Association, San Antonio, Texas. Retrieved from www.youtube.com/watch?v=0qbGoo0N0lU

Liu, K. K., Ward, J. M., Thurlow, M. L., & Christensen, L. L. (2017). Large-scale assessment and English language learners with disabilities. *Educational Policy, 31*(5), 551–583.

Marsh, K. (2019, March 27). Looking through many eyes: Evaluating students' empathy using written expression. Paper presented at Community of Scholars Day, Lesley University, Cambridge, MA.

Miller, R. D. (2016). Contextualizing instruction for English language learners with learning disabilities. *Teaching Exceptional Children, 49(1),* 58–65. Retrieved from https://doi.org/10.1177/0040059916662248

Newton, C., & Wilson, D. (2003). *Creating circles of friends. A peer support and inclusion workbook.* Nottingham, England: Inclusive Solutions UK Limited.

Petrina, N., Carter, M., & Stephenson, J. (2014). The nature of friendship in children with autism spectrum disorders: A systematic review. *Research in Autism Spectrum Disorders, 8,* 111–126. doi:10.1016/j.rasd.2013.10.016

Rance-Roney, J. (2008). Creating intentional communities to support English language learners in the classroom. *English Journal, 97*(5), 17–22.

Rossetti, Z., Ross, J., & Brennen, M. A. (2017). *Making friends with and without disabilities in school: A toolkit for teachers, paraprofessionals, and parents.* Waltham, MA: The Arc of Massachusetts. Retrieved from thearcofmass.org/wp-content/uploads/2015/12/FRIENDSHIP-TOOLKIT-DIGITAL-PDF-rev-marc-26-2017.pdf

Rossetti, Z., Sauer, J. S., Bui, O., & Ou, S. (2017). Developing collaborative partnerships with culturally and linguistically diverse families during the IEP process. *Teaching Exceptional Children, 48*(5), 328–338.

Santillan, Y., Jacobs, J. M., & Wright, P. M. (2015). Integrating best practices in ELL classrooms with quality physical education instruction. *Journal of Physical Education, Recreation & Dance, 86*(3), 51–53. Retrieved from www.tandfonline.com/doi/abs/10.1080/07303084.2015.998553

Serpa, M. (2019). *An imperative for change: Bridging special and language learning education to ensure a free and appropriate education in the least restrictive environment for ELLs with disabilities in Massachusetts.* Boston, MA: University of Massachusetts, Gastón Institute Publications.

Slama, R., Molefe, A., Gerdeman, D., Herrera, A., Brodziak de los Reyes, I., August, D., & Cavazos, L. (2017). *Time to proficiency for Hispanic English learner students in Texas* (REL 2018-280). Washington, DC: U.S. Department of Education, Institute of Education Sciences, National Center for Education Evaluation and Regional Assistance, Regional Educational Laboratory Southwest. Retrieved from ies.ed.gov/ncee/edlabs/regions/southwest/pdf/REL_2018280.pdf

Stepanek, J., Raphael, J., Autio, E., Deussen, T., & Thompson, L. (2010). Creating schools that support success for English language learners. *Lessons Learned, 1*(2). Retrieved from files.eric.ed.gov/fulltext/ED519412.pdf

Tervalon, M., & Murray-Garcia, J. (1998). Cultural humility versus cultural competence: A critical distinction in defining physician training outcomes in multicultural education. *Journal of Health Care for the Poor and Undeserved, 9,* 117–125

Tipton, L. A., Christensen, L., & Blacher, J. (2013). Friendship quality in adolescents with and without an intellectual disability. *Journal of Applied Research in Intellectual Disabilities, 26,* 522–532. doi:10.1111/jar.12051

Turnbull, A., Turnbull, R., Erwin, E. J., Soodak, L. C., & Shogren, K. A. (2011). *Families, professionals, and exceptionality: Positive outcomes through partnership and trust.* Boston, MA: Pearson.

Van Der Klift, E., & Kunc, N. (2019). *Being realistic isn't realistic: Collected essays on disability, identity, inclusion and innovation.* Victoria, BC, Canada: Tellwell Talent.

Index

About the Authors

Janet Story Sauer is a professor of special education in the College of Liberal Arts and Professional Studies at Lesley University in Cambridge, MA. She taught children in Botswana, Africa, on the Navajo Reservation, and in Boston, Ohio, and Iowa. At the university, Sauer co-teaches with people with disabilities, their family members, and guests from other disciplines to illustrate the complex and interdisciplinary nature of disability. She has published research articles, book chapters, and a book of portraits about children with significant support needs. Her research interests focus on examining positive relationships in inclusive contexts, the nature of creativity as access to literacy, and interdisciplinary collaboration. Sauer's advocacy efforts for the inclusion of students with disabilities in community and educational contexts have also led her to explore co-constructions in portraiture research methodology.

Zach Rossetti is an associate professor of special education in the Boston University Wheelock College of Education & Human Development. A former elementary school special education teacher and inclusion facilitator from New Hampshire, Rossetti's research focuses on the experiences of families with children with intellectual and developmental disabilities (IDD) or autism spectrum disorder (ASD) by centering on family–school collaboration and community participation, as well as sibling roles and relationships. His research also examines social interactions and friendships between students with and without IDD in inclusive settings, specifically the contexts and dynamics of such relationships and how educators may facilitate social interactions and friendship opportunities. Rossetti is on the editorial board of *Intellectual and Developmental Disabilities* and *Research and Practice for Persons with Severe Disabilities*. He is co-author of *Seeing the Charade: What We Need to Do and Undo to Make Friendships Happen* (2006).